THE ART
OF COLLABORATION

THE ART
OF COLLABORATION

The Real Truth
About Working Well
With Others

Jo Ann Romero

iUniverse, Inc.

New York Bloomington Shanghai

The Art Of Collaboration
The Real Truth About Working Well With Others

iUniverse books may be ordered through booksellers or by contacting:

iUniverse
1663 Liberty Drive
Bloomington, IN 47403
www.iuniverse.com
1-800-Authors (1-800-288-4677)

Because of the dynamic nature of the Internet, any Web addresses or links contained in this book may have changed since publication and may no longer be valid.

The views expressed in this work are solely those of the author and do not necessarily reflect the views of the publisher, and the publisher hereby disclaims any responsibility for them.

ISBN: 978-0-595-44719-0 (pbk)
ISBN: 978-0-595-68960-6 (cloth)
ISBN: 978-0-595-89040-8 (ebk)

Printed in the United States of America

This book is dedicated to the circle of those in my life from which the essence of true meaning lie. To my husband David, whose support and encouragement never falter. To Karen whose unending care, authenticity, and generosity still inspire everything good and whose love and legacy lives on deep inside my heart and soul. To Rita whose courage, gentleness, friendship and love sustain my life. To the little children to whom we owe living examples of cooperation, compassion and empathy. To Sofia and Thomas whose innocence and hopefulness require us all to find a way to leave this world better. Finally, to my precious mom and dad who brought us up to believe that any endeavor conceived in the heart and fueled by faith and hard work is possible.

Contents

1

The Cry for Collaboration

○ ○

As iron sharpens iron,
so one man sharpens another.

—Proverbs 27:17

Why is it that with the best of intentions, bright, hardworking people throw up their hands in frustration and give up on the idea of working with important partners even when the potential gain is compelling? What is that tendency we have to distrust those we don't know and to assume hidden agendas?

For more years than I care to remember, these questions have continued to frustrate me and many of my colleagues. As I reflect on the many years working with those questions, I've witnessed the great mystery slowly unravel. I have experimented, watched my experiments work well and, frankly, not so well at times, and then began to see patterns emerge.

My reason for writing this book is fairly straightforward. I've felt frustration watching what seemed to be tremendous opportunity for collaboration and gain dissipate into lethargic circular meetings that went nowhere. I've also been present when the magic of vision came alive, when ideas grew bigger and better with input, and when the results were more than could have been imagined at the start. My intention for writing this book is to share my hard-earned and very practical wisdom and tools that I've gathered or created along the way.

The knowledge I offer is based on years of working across the country designing and facilitating countless interactions between both friends and foes. If a single reader finds even a single kernel or nugget to apply and use with his own efforts, then taking the time to write this book has been worth doing.

Over time, I have developed a few strong biases. One is that when collaboration works, the solutions are better, sharper, and more meaningful. When synergy happens and the sum of the result expands beyond what the individual parts could have done, the energy, commitment, enthusiasm, buy-in, and implementation never fail to satisfy.

It is important to keep this fundamental truth in front of us as we think about why we continue to pursue this commingling of talent, ideas, and energy. It is not because we have to, or because we should, it is because the issues we face today are unprecedented in their complexity and challenge. We need synergy, and we need our solutions to be sharper, more inclusive, and more meaningful.

My job in helping to birth collaborations is to enable my clients to make something larger, better, and stronger out of what they start with. The work I've been involved with over the past twenty years has allowed me to experience both ends and everywhere along the spectrum of frustration to brilliance and from average success to astounding results.

The journey continues. In spite of the challenge, the human spirit seeking synergy and better, more efficient, lasting, and sustainable solutions to all kinds of issues continues to fuel the search for success in collaboration. As we continue to learn about what works and where problems arise, the patterns become more visible, and what is required of those attempting to work in this new way becomes clearer. As this awareness grows, we continue incorporating lessons learned into our workshops and facilitations. This book is about those insights and patterns and what the reader needs to know and do and be to get to those astounding results.

As I continue to work, I gather, develop, test, and refine my models and constructs, and then I use them, test them, and refine them again. I offer these models and constructs with the intention of assisting you in working toward the goal of mutual satisfaction and gain with your partners and potential partners. Writing this down and sharing it seemed to be the next step along this journey, and we welcome your feedback and refinements back to me.

Just outside of my personal orbit, it seems everyone is realizing just how important collaboration is as a way of doing business now and increasingly so in the future. What is less obvious is what specific capacities and skills are required to bring people, interests, and issues to the table and what it takes to cocreate mutually satisfying solutions and opportunities.

Much effort has been spent trying to define collaboration, partnerships, alliances, joint ventures, working together in any way. I've happened upon at least ten different definitions, from Webster's to the more convoluted org-speak. Some are scholarly in nature; others are sharp and to the point. What I've done is to think of collaboration in as straightforward a way as possible. To that end, I offer this simple definition: collaboration is the *movement of value between parties.* As I see it, anytime two or more parties exchange what they consider to be valuable, collaboration occurs.

This book explores how that *movement of value* between parties can happen in as smooth, efficient, painless, and effective a way as possible. The word "painless" may have evoked a grin. If you have labored with collaborative efforts, I suspect you are only too well aware of how painful those long, ethereal meetings can be.

As we move into the book, let me start by clearing up a few notions about what collaboration is not. Much to my surprise, when I first began teaching workshops on collaboration, I found myself struggling with the definition. It seems a few World War II–veteran students took umbrage to the term "collaboration." It seems the word had very specific meaning during the war, and it was not favorable. Being referred to as "collaborator" was tantamount to being called a traitor!

Considering that era and the meaning of the word at that time, I wonder if in some way that particular definition didn't set the stage for what was to follow. Let me explain. After World War II, most American organizations were proud to be independent, strong, fierce, and competitive. To share information or to work with competitors was unthinkable. To do so was viewed as dangerous, disloyal, risky, and clearly a sign of weakness. Besides, after the war, it was completely unnecessary. After all, business was booming, and there really was enough to go around. If a company needed something, they expanded. Trade secrets were fiercely protected; people in the same business were viewed as potential enemies.

Is it any wonder that those notions still haunt the corridors of many large organizations today? To some extent, the residue of that kind of thinking is still lurking. The hesitancy to admit mistakes, share doubt, or candidly discuss uncertainty about how things are done or should be done seems to be alive and well in many of today's organizations.

Control, consistency, and stability were the hallmarks of that era. The model of organizations as machinery was popular, and it gave a lot of authority to the large cogs in the wheel. We expected decision makers to do the thinking, do the right thing, and tell the rest of us where to go and how to get there. Respect for authority was the norm. To challenge decisions or to suggest that there might be a different or better way to do things was just not done. Respect and deference to authority was the order of the day. Aahh, the good old days!

Consider the post–World War II era compared to present day. The contrast is startling. Who among us now has the depth of knowledge, technology, insight, and resources to do everything ourselves? Which of us can truly say we understand the complexities, implications, and operating environment well enough to invest our limited resources without consulting others? How many of us know what lurks ahead and can confidently plan on exactly how we should move ahead?

Over the past fifteen years or so, the dynamics of organizations have changed so much that our heads spin. While most of us grew up prizing our independence and striving to become more and more independent, the marketplace and the ambiguity and complexity of our current workplace scream for us to be interdependent.

The shift from trusting and respecting those in charge to automatic distrust is more the norm now and has strong implications for how we work. The line between organizations and industries is completely blurred. Information is available anytime, anywhere, to anyone who seeks to find it.

Technology and instant access have sped up expectations such that once a question is asked, there is someone needing an answer immediately. Not having the time to think things through or look at all sides of an issue begs for having access to solid, reliable networks of people who can look deeply at their piece of the puzzle and offer input to our work and decisions.

Then there is the issue of expectations. While we're not exactly sure when as a nation or as individuals the bar of expectations was raised to its current level, we know it has been raised. If you watch trends, you may have noted the five-minute drive-through shoe repair business, or the offer of buying your new car online but not before zooming in on a large image of that car in different colors or seat upholstery options! We have high expectations. Our bosses, constituents, and customers have high expectations, and our children's expectations are even higher. Let's translate that to the workplace.

The public expects to be involved in decisions that affect them and their communities. As the baby boomer generation retires, hold on. Their expectations surrounding recreational needs, community expansion or preservation, and what type of communities they want will skyrocket.

Employees expect to know what is happening and where their leaders are taking them. Customers expect to have access to your plans and how their needs figure into the equation. We are expected to integrate services, communication, information, and access, and to provide system solutions to all kinds of problems. As we work with multiple constituencies, our own capacity is limited, and oh, by the way, most customers and publics don't much care about organizational lines.

For example, community members who are facing the invasion of developers or unplanned migrations want support to manage growth from their officials. As far as they are concerned, whether the decisions need to come from the Park Service, the Forest Service, the Bureau of Land Management, or the state or county officials makes no difference. In the mind of the community members, you are all the same.

What that translates to is the need for the federal, state, and local officials to cooperate, have the same story, a set of shared objectives, and to be a single mouthpiece for issue resolution and decisions. Unfortunately, that's not how it typically works. People are frustrated with having to work with endless bureaucracy and red tape, the results of which are too often misunderstanding, hostility, lost time, limited or no progress, and court battles.

Private business that needs to move fast and doesn't have the time or capital to do it all has to be smart about its investments and about its partners. We have to get savvy about who to trust and how to go about developing fruitful networks.

For internal organizations who offer service, we can no longer survive by providing transactions. We have to offer something better. To become a true partner with your customers internally is to enliven your existence and bring value to what you do.

As you can see, collaboration in these times is not a luxury or something nice to do. It is an absolute mandate, necessary as never before. As you read on, I implore you to open your mind and focus on how to let go of this notion that we are independent. We need each other. Our customers and our neighbors need us to work together. It's time to reframe how we think about our competitors. It's time to let go of this notion that we must have more resources—more employees to do the work, more specialists, more capability.

Instead, I challenge you to think about how you can leverage what you have, how you can create networks of loyalty and capacity and how you can set up shared interests in such a way that what's in it for each party is explicit and out in the open and there is a shared commitment to the success of the whole.

This journey may not be easy, but I promise it will be enlightening and fruitful.

2

This is the Hard Stuff:
Common Traps and Pitfalls

○ ○
It is not good to have zeal without knowledge
nor to be hasty and miss the way.

—Proverbs 19:2

If you buy the argument that partnering is the only way through the present organizational morass, then why is it so hard? I know many bright, hardworking, well-intentioned individuals who know they need to partner with others both inside and outside their own functional areas and organizations. Their glossy strategic plans go on about partnering with communities, friends, and foes to manage the land and the plethora of other issues. They are told that partnering is a key priority and focus for the future. It is not unusual to operate under legal mandate that requires engaging in participative practices.

Others want to bid on lucrative contracts and know it would be impossible given the time constraints to go it alone. If they want to win this contract, they have to find partners.

A good, long-term, loyal customer asks you to partner with another supplier—a competitor—to deliver a product quickly. What to do?

This thing is bigger than we are. Everywhere you look, individuals and companies large and small are working to engage with others. If we only had that all-important idea or technology—a breakthrough! Complexity is rampant. The luxury of working in contained systems is a thing of the past. Money is tight. Competition is everywhere. Most of us can't afford to do everything ourselves, and those customers sure are demanding! This is not a new phenomenon, but what to do with it all is the question.

Let's be frank. It would be easier to do things ourselves. It might even be more efficient if we could just go about our business, make decisions as needed, tell the customers what they need—and move on.

We've already discussed the fact that things are different. The market, the forces in the external environment, and the general set of expectations are requiring that we take collaboration seriously.

Let's not paint it anyway but how it really is. There are many pitfalls and common traps. There are many good reasons to throw up your hands in frustration.

After working in this arena for many years, stepping on a few landmines and collecting information from others about what their common traps and pitfalls are, I offer the following list of twenty pitfalls and errors you should pay attention to and work to avoid making. Following the list, I have considered each of the pitfalls separately and provided ideas and anecdotes for avoiding or mitigating these common traps.

Use this list as a checklist for assessing the condition of your collaborative efforts, particularly if they appear to be stalled.

Pitfalls and Common Errors

1. Not taking the time to do an intentionally focused start-up

2. Trying to move too fast (focusing on efficiency versus effectiveness)

3. Failing to discover who your fellow partners are, what they might gain by participating in the effort, what they want and/or what they need from the effort

4. Failing to disclose your intentions

5. Underestimating the time required to build rapport, trust, and relationship

6. Failing to seek and find common ground

7. Failing to set a clear and shared vision and context for what you are doing

8. Advocating a position before you fully understand all aspects of the situation

9. Believing your way, or the way things have always been done, is the only way

10. Making and acting on assumptions that have not been validated

11. Lacking clear roles and responsibilities for the collaborative effort

12. Lacking specificity about what your organization is hoping to achieve as a result of the collaborative effort

13. Planning poorly

14. Lacking a shared vision

15. Allowing unhealthy egos to get in the way

16. Clashing of cultures

17. Lacking realistic expectations/milestones

18. Lacking collaborative expertise/leadership

19. Lacking follow-through

20. Failing to engage adequate involvement and support of key decision makers

As you consider each of the common errors separately, think about situations you have been involved with and whether they might have been more successful if you could have avoided or resolved these pitfalls.

1. Not taking the time to do an intentionally focused start-up

Let me share a bias here. When all is said and done, I have internalized this one thing. If people would do a well planned, intentional, focused start-up, the world of collaborative efforts would become easier and better overnight.

There is no way to overstate the importance of doing the first part with great thought and care. When the effort goes south or frustration is rampant, it can be tracked back to the start-up nearly every time. A few questions to ask yourself as you begin:

- Have you carefully considered who should be included and at the table?

- Have you adequately analyzed what you know about those coming to the table?

- Have you considered the history of the relationship and have you created a specific set of strategies for dealing with the relationships?

- If there are major gaps in what you know about your potential partner(s), have you planned time to discover what you need to know prior to the first meeting?

- Who could be impacted by this effort? Who could help it along? Who might view the effort as controversial or be an adversary? Are there individuals or organizations that could influence the outcome? Who could stop or block the effort?

- Have you considered the tone you want to set and what, if any, leadership should be present at the start to validate the overall organizational commitment to pursue the effort?

- Have you erred on the side of inclusion at least for the start-up?

- Have you carefully considered the ability of the person in charge of the start-up? Are they the best technical expert and do they have an affinity to listen? Do they have a demonstrated record of keeping an open mind? How do they tend to deal with conflict and challenging personalities?

- Have you allowed adequate time for establishing rapport and building relationship?

- Is the agenda clear, and are the outcomes for the meeting clearly stated? Does the agenda reflect the needs and desires of all of those participating?

- Have you clarified your intention for the effort and for the relationship, and are you ready to share your intention with the group?

- What is your plan for finding and clearly articulating whatever common ground exists between parties?

- Have you intentionally set the stage for a thorough exploration of possibilities?

- Are you prepared to clearly state what your organization is hoping to achieve as a result of this effort? Have you clearly stated your willingness to be open and do what makes sense for everyone at the table?

- Are you willing to truly suspend or set aside your position in the interest of exploring possibilities and options?

- Have you done adequate preparation with participants ahead of time so that they know what to expect when they come together?

- Have you considered inviting a co-sponsor of the effort from the other side? Have you thought about how the leadership, planning, and execution of the meetings might be shared?

- Have you considered using a third-party facilitator who can be neutral and take an objective view of the process?

- Have you positioned the first meeting(s) as an exploration in which the group can consider whether to proceed?

As you can see, there is a lot to consider. The planning and thoughtful execution of the initial contact will pay big dividends. If you don't have time to do the beginning well, consider delaying it until you can do it right.

2. Trying to move too fast (focusing on efficiency versus effectiveness)

Today's pace is frantic. With so much to do, most of us need to feel we are making progress minute by minute. We want to check off the items on our "to do" list. We want that rush of accomplishment associated with getting things done and being efficient.

As it turns out, real collaboration is generally not efficient. In fact, it can even be somewhat messy and take more time than we typically plan for. It should not be surprising to us that strangers coming together, even when interests are common, are not likely to move forward in a linear way. Why then do we tend to plan them as if they were linear? If indeed the first meeting were to move too efficiently or without any question, we ought to be suspicious. Do people feel comfortable enough to be authentic and honest about what is on their minds?

Rather than feel frustrated, push too hard, or promise to deliver results in an unrealistic time frame, it is better to adequately plan up front for the time you will actually need.

Remember, it takes time to bring people together, to understand why people are there, what your collective views about the situation are, what you each want, what you need, and what the individual and collective benefit of pursuing the effort might be.

Over time, I have experienced the richest results when a group starts out intentionally open to what may or may not unfold.

It is not unusual for the up-front start-up phase to take six to eight months. When I hear someone spouting their schedule for designing and working through a partnership or collaboration in the next ninety days, I tend to wish them a miracle.

Do not be taken in by the false economy of efficiency versus effectiveness.

3. Failing to discover who your fellow partners are, what they might gain by participating in the effort, what they want and/or need from the effort

In my humble view, the single most common reason for collaborative efforts failing to meet their intended result or stalling out is a lack of clarity about where each party is coming from and what each is going to gain from their participation.

It seems most people enter collaborative efforts with a good idea about what *they* (or their organization) want or stand to gain. Too often the person starting up the effort is persuasive, articulate, and has very clear ideas about where this effort should go. When blank stares, or argument, fail to meet their persuasive arguments, they back up and repeat their ideas again—and again. It's as if they think that if they could just say it correctly or use the right words, the other parties would "get it."

What has become obvious is that it is here at the *beginning* that one must enter the exchange with the true spirit of exploration. Explorers don't already know the answer; they are seeking, feeling their way, learning about the terrain, expecting the unexpected.

There is a need for the convener to be genuinely curious about whether there is something in it for each player to proceed and about whether or not it makes sense to everyone to proceed. It is impossible to know this unless you are willing to listen, seek to understand, walk in the others' shoes, examine issues, and lighten the grip on your own position.

David Boehm, a nuclear physicist at the Los Alamos National Laboratory who worked on the Manhattan Project back in the 1940s, did some important work in an attempt to understand how the human mind works. His work was driven by a desire to find out what it takes to get to breakthrough thinking, a particularly important aspect of the Manhattan Project. Peter Senge, who discusses the same notion of how the mind works in his Ladder of Inference, later adapted Boehm's work.

The essence of the work done on the Ladder of Inference is that without conscious thought, each of us walks around observing data rather like recording on a movie camera. As we observe data, we make assumptions about what we observe; we add meaning to those assumptions, adopt beliefs, and then act on those beliefs. This is critically important to understand, because this process occurs without our thoughtful, conscious consideration about what beliefs we are carrying around or whether those beliefs are valid. What we believe about our potential partners will impact how we behave toward them and how we interact with them and ultimately the results of our effort. For example, if I assume that my partners will only try to satisfy their own wants, it is doubtful that I will truly open up to what they have to say or what they might suggest. If I adopt the belief that collaboration takes too much time with little payoff, my actions will reflect that assumption and my beliefs become self-fulfilling.

The work of both Boehm and Senge is enormously relevant to successful collaboration because it clearly illustrates how we unconsciously limit breakthrough thinking because of our well-cemented mental models and beliefs about how things *should* work. We carry around our sack of assumptions even when they weigh us down and limit our progress.

The very best collaborative efforts happen when the participants take on an attitude of discovery. It is only when we suspend our assumptions and open ourselves to the reality that we just can't know everything that we are able to set aside our own knowledge and look for and listen at a very deep level. It is at this level that the magic begins to happen.

4. Failing to disclose your intentions

Earlier on, I discussed the human tendency to distrust what we don't know. We can assume that there is some value to distrusting what we don't know and that it may be a part of our survival instinct. When it comes to collaboration, however, we must be explicit and intentional about where we are starting from. That is, we can start from the premise that there will be no trust of my partners until they prove that they can be trusted, or we can start from the premise that they are trustworthy and will be trusted until they prove themselves untrustworthy. These are very different starting points.

Beginning from the premise that my partners can be trusted until they violate that trust makes more sense and is much more conducive to real collaboration.

Trust is nebulous; it is typically hard fought and easily lost. One of the best ways I know to begin the walk toward gaining the trust of others is to be very clear about your intentions. Are you open to sharing what your intent is? Do you take the time to set context for what you say? Do people know what is behind your positions? If the answer is no, then expect it will be harder and take longer.

5. Underestimating the time required to build rapport, trust, and relationship

Humans are naturally nervous in certain situations. One situation that causes us tension and discomfort is coming together with people whom we know nothing about, or whom we know don't agree with us, our organization, or what we stand for. The discomfort we feel tends to make us want to get to safe ground as quickly as possible. In collaborative efforts, that safe ground is typically the problem that needs to be resolved.

This desire for safety plays out as we go around the room and introduce ourselves and then jump quickly to dissecting the problem more minutely or even to trying to solve the problem.

The thing to remember is that people can't do business with you unless they know who you are, what you stand for, and whether their trust is well placed with you.

Once you internalize this fact, you are on your way to understanding that you must take the time to step back, listen, converse, find areas of mutual interest, build rapport, and disclose who you are and what your intentions are. It is when you express genuine interest in your fellow humans that the seeds for successful collaboration are sowed.

Last—this is hard—can you afford what might be called a waste of time? That is, can you live with taking hours, maybe days, and certainly more than one meeting, to build a relationship? Just know that the very foundation of your collaborative efforts depends on it.

6. Failing to seek and find common ground

Think about those people in your life that you are closest to. Think about your relationships and the comfort and affinity that exists between you and those you are closest to and most comfortable with. It is highly likely that those closest to you have much in common with you. That is, your beliefs, interests, values, and habits are likely to overlap significantly. What you have in common is shared beliefs and perhaps history.

Think about what it is like to sit with strangers. Based on what you know at the start, there is no affinity. The challenge then is to engage with people long enough and sincerely enough to find out what you have in common. It might be as simple as a shared interest in the outdoors, having lived in the same part of the country, or a shared disdain for gas prices!

I remember a particular meeting where it was clear there needed to be better collaboration between a group of oil and gas industry players and a public organization that approved their permits to drill. The first time they sat face-to-face is hard to forget.

The atmosphere was thick with anticipation and tension. The public officials and the oil representatives had disagreed on many points over many years. There had been angry letters and threats bandied back and forth. Getting them to come together had taken a lot of effort and convincing. The moment arrived. As the oil men (yes, all men) entered the room, jaws were tight, handshakes were firm and fast.

To start the meeting, and to their complete surprise, I asked them to introduce themselves and to indicate the part of the country they most enjoyed and why. By the end of that round of introductions, real laughter, stories, and lots of commonalities replaced the nervous laughter.

After continued discussion, it became clear that what they really had in common was a deep desire to preserve or at least not harm the drill beds. In spite of their differences, there was something real that they had in common. That single issue served as the anchor for the remainder of the effort.

Don't leave these things to chance. Take the time to set up the process to ensure the exploration includes the opportunity to find common ground.

7. Failing to set a clear and shared vision and context for what you are doing

It's been said that effective collaboration occurs when there is a balance of relationship, context, and procedure. Let me analyze this further. Relationship is clearly the apex of your collaboration. Without it and the resultant trust, the effort is likely to go nowhere or to fall short of the intended result.

The context for the collaborative effort is equally important. That is, what is the reason for the effort? When the going gets tough, what is the anchor that holds it together and calls you back on course? Another way to say it is what is the compelling business case for the effort?

While it may sound obvious, what I have discovered is that too often groups move forward with a context that belongs to a certain individual or there are numerous contexts. What is called for is a single, clear, compelling, shared context.

In order to get to that context, consider what you are trying to achieve, why you are trying to achieve it, and how it will benefit both the customer and each participant.

An example to illustrate this concept is one that was relatively difficult from the start. The relationship had a long history of dissent, and there had been many false starts over the years. Individuals in charge had changed regularly over time, and there was little trust that this time around would be any different.

The new leader and sponsor was a charismatic, energetic, visionary kind of person. He seemed to have a natural curiosity and was a great listener. The first several meetings were spent exploring who the players were, what brought them to the table, and what they had in common.

It was clear that the relationship was on its way to being created and that it wouldn't be long before a mutual trust developed. Once that was established, the tone gently turned toward deciding what their collective best hopes were for this effort.

After what seemed like a long time, people began to define what success would mean to them and what their individual criteria for success would be.

Not until they gave much thoughtful consideration did the group hone in on what they referred to as their business case for the effort. They had defined a shared context for what they would pursue. That same context would serve them again and again. As new players came onboard, when obstacles appeared, when relationships became frayed, they went back to the context and reminded themselves what the struggle was about and why they were willing to work through whatever complexities they faced.

8. Advocating a position before you fully understand all aspects of the situation

Taking a firm position too soon in a collaborative situation is a dangerous thing with potentially high consequence. What underlies firm positions is an implied statement of "I'm right" or "I know best."

The problems with putting the advocacy stake in the ground too soon are many. Once you take a firm position, it is harder to change it. It makes it harder to save face. You begin to get identified by your position. The impact is divisive. If you are not careful, camps form: the camp that agrees with you and the one that doesn't. Divisiveness has no place in collaboration.

To avoid this pitfall, hold your position in abeyance. If that is too hard, consider: Am I operating with an open attitude? Am I truly willing to find the best solution even if it turns out to be different from what I think I want? If the answer is no, reexamine your attitude. If the answer is yes, hold on. The group's wisdom will eventually see what you already know, or the best solution will surface. Once that happens, you can be assured that true collaboration has occurred.

Just as we admire the rare leader who gathers all of the available information before making a decision, we also admire the party at the table who does the same.

9. Believing your way, or the way it has always been done is, the only way

A particular collaborative scenario comes to mind here. It was a situation every bit as difficult as it was memorable. From the start, there was an undercurrent of angst. The parties were together because they had to be. Large dollars were at stake. A high-level city official had been pressured to ensure some of the money for this particular high-dollar construction project was shared with a small-business entity.

The large firm who had been selected as the prime contractor for the award of the project was very large, experienced, and quite successful. The small firm who had won the subcontract was torn between excitement about being included and fear of being consumed by the large company.

The setting for the launch of the effort was tense. As they worked to get to know each other and identify what they needed individually to ensure success, the issue of payments and how and when they would be made during performance of the contract came up.

The individual from the city responsible for paying the contractors said in a very firm and knowing way that payments would be made as normal. They would issue payment to the prime contractor and they could expect a thirty to forty-five day payment cycle. The prime contractor nodded in agreement.

By chance, I happened to notice a look of terror cross the face of the small contractor. Making a point to make space for her to speak, I asked her whether that payment cycle would work for her. Before she could speak, the prime contractor jumped in to say that if their payment cycle was forty-five days, the small contractor could expect another fifteen to thirty days for them to process payment down to them.

For the small company, this was a deal breaker. The woman representing the small firm, in a steady but nervous voice, indicated that they would not able to float their payroll for that amount of time. Since they planned to devote most of their resources to performance of this contract, the impact of the slow payment cycle could literally put them out of business.

The city official representing the financial area repeated over and over again that there was nothing they could do. Their payment process was set in stone, and there was no alternative. If there was a solution, this person did not have it.

After sharing her long list of endless reasons for why nothing could change, and about the time it looked like the deal was off, the financial representative from the prime contractor began to offer possibilities for how they might work their internal system to move payments through to the subcontractor more quickly. The prime contractor had entered into a problem-solving mode in the interest of saving the contract from disaster.

The lesson here is that one individual was absolutely convinced that there was no alternative. She truly believed that the way they processed payments was the only way it could ever be done. From her perspective, it was black and white. It was not until another stepped up and expressed a willingness to explore the shades of gray that the entire, multimillion dollar effort was saved.

By the end of the meeting, it was clear that having the conversation openly and early had prevented disaster. How many assumptions do we make about how things will work? In this case, a transition meeting and having a collaborative forum to dissect how things would work and dialogue about various ways to do things made a huge difference.

10. Making and acting on assumptions that have not been validated

Assumptions are limiting. I want to remind you what happens when we make assumptions. First, it is normal and part of being human. As it turns out, it is really a survival mechanism. If we enter a room, see that there is a stove over in the corner and that there is a burning flame emanating from the stove, we automatically assume that stove is hot. Let's say that we have a two-year-old in tow. It is important that the instant assumption activates since we are surely going to turn off the burner or make sure that toddler does not get close to the flame. In that instance, the assumption serves the situation well.

In a collaborative effort, however, that same mechanism can get us into trouble. To illustrate this point, I will address a real situation.

A vice president representing a midsize technology firm contacted the owner of a small tech start-up firm to set up a meeting. All the small firm knew was that the midsize firm was considering working with them and indicated that there might be mutual benefit. During the conversation, the midsized firm indicated that they were looking for ways to satisfy a need of one of their customers and the name of the small firm had been mentioned as a potential source for a certain technology.

After receiving the initial call to request a meeting, the owner of the small firm began to ponder what might be up. "This more-established, well-known company wants to work with us. What could they want? Perhaps they are trying to find out who our customers are so that they can make an end run. Suppose that this is a fishing expedition to learn what they can about our portfolio. Who is this person anyway, and what does her company really want? She seemed a little too slick—something must be awry."

At the first meeting, the small company owner found himself sitting across the table from the woman who made the initial contact with him. The owner told me later that he felt a little cool and protective about what he said. They had after all worked hard to be a very independent, small, but successful firm. Why would he disclose any of his plans to this person?

In a snap, assumptions overtook him. Assumptions about what the initiating firm wanted and about what he might lose as a result of the interaction. The result of adopting those beliefs was that he approached the meeting ensconced in a cool demeanor, protective about what he said. Without suspending his suspicions, he had come to the table assuming many things—most of which were negative. How do you think his behavior and approach might impact possibilities?

We know that in the absence of valid information, people tend to fill in the blanks. And, unfortunately, those blanks tend to run toward the negative.

In this same situation, it may well have been that there was potential for mutual gain and that indeed there was potential for significant value for both parties. What is the likelihood that the value would be realized with his unstated and invalidated assumptions in the way?

My intention here is to try to illustrate how, in an instant, we can limit our possibilities because of the assumptions, beliefs, and actions based on those beliefs we make without thinking or challenging what we believe.

Play back the scenario again. What if it went this way? Let's say that when the owner of the small high-tech firm put the phone back in the cradle after receiving the initial request, he intentionally decided to take the request at face value. Perhaps he did a little homework to find out who the other company was and began thinking about what he might learn from them. Let's suppose he decided he would engage them in an open and candid way with the intention of learning something.

He might have found the cost of partnering with the other firm wasn't worth the potential payoff. Or he might have determined that it was a worthwhile pursuit. By listening openly and with the intent to learn and understand, he might have developed a new relationship with a colleague and perhaps made a useful contact for the future—and that's the worst case.

One more tip on this subject. Be explicit and intentional to become aware of your assumptions. Take exquisite care not to jump too quickly to act on those assumptions. Be willing to set aside your assumptions in order to learn what others are offering you. You can always take your assumptions back! Our mental models serve us, but they can also get in the way.

11. Lacking clear roles and responsibilities for the collaborative effort.

Earlier I said that the most effective collaborative efforts are where there is a balance between relationship, context, and procedure. What we're talking about here is part of that third element or the procedures that clearly specify how the collaborative process will work. This includes the process, the logistics, the way you intend to manage the meetings, how you will handle conflict, and how you will determine roles and responsibilities.

A key to remember here is that the procedures are important and it is necessary to have someone paying attention to them. While you are in the process of building trust, it is particularly important to have an organized approach and a method for communicating.

Once you have set the stage for the collaborative effort to proceed, it is time to think about who will do what. I think it is important for the sponsor/convener to be clear at the outset about what his or her role is. For example, are you there as the technical expert or is your role during the meeting to facilitate the session—or both? Don't leave people to speculate about what you are doing. Let people know what your role is and what your role is likely to be in the future. If your leadership is present at the beginning, let the participants know what their role is and how much participation and input they can expect to have throughout the process.

It generally works best when the group decides who will take the notes, when the next meeting will be, who will set up the following meetings, etc.

Look for opportunity to engage your partners in taking an active role in the success of the effort. Ask them what role they want to play and what they need from you in support of that role.

Expect the procedures to evolve. At the end of meetings, ask people whether there is clarity about what happened and what will happen next. Summarize agreements and areas that the group is still addressing. Encourage the group to remain flexible and to rotate responsibilities and roles.

Encourage the group to think through how disagreements and conflict will be handled. Will everyone have the role of identifying when there appears to be discord? What procedure will be used to resolve issues as they arise? How much intervention from your leadership should the group expect, and when will that happen?

Lastly, having good procedures and clear roles will not make the collaboration effective. However, not having procedures or clarity about who is responsible for what will cause confusion and can lead to loss in interest, commitment, and frustration.

12. Lacking specificity about what your organization is hoping to achieve as a result of the collaborative effort

This topic makes me think back many, many years to one of the first collaborative efforts I was responsible for designing and facilitating. My client, the sponsor of the effort, had painted a fairly grim portrait about what to expect. He and the potential partner were longtime competitors who shared a customer. The customer had approached my client to tell him that they were no longer going to tolerate the negative comments they were hearing from his people about the other player and would be telling their competitor the same.

This savvy customer had decided that he or she was likely to be the beneficiary of synergy if these two longtime competitors worked together to meet customer needs versus wasting time working against each other as they had been.

My client viewed the call from the customer as a veiled threat, and he was in no position to lose or disenfranchise his long-term, important customer.

I remember how much planning went into that first meeting. I remember speaking with several of the participants from both sides prior to the meeting. Everyone was nervous and understood only too well what the ramification might be if their attempt to work together failed.

We carefully considered the best location for the meeting—neutral ground, of course. The morning of the first session, I remember walking up to the front of the room. You could have cut the atmosphere with a knife. I noticed that along one side of the long table, several people from one side sat stiffly lined up close together. On the other side was the other set of stiff, suited people nearly huddled together.

I knew that the first words were important. The tone would be set by what was said.

I noticed that the chairs were blue. I made some comment about blue being a neutral, conciliatory color and asked them to focus on the blue if things got rough. Nervous laughter broke the ice.

During the introductions, I asked people to indicate what their respective organizations were trying to achieve in both the long-term strategic sense and in the more near term.

Looking back, I realize by encouraging them to start by thinking more globally about what their organizations were trying to achieve, they were better able to put the presenting issue into a bigger context.

The group spent the first several hours learning from one another about what their organizations were trying to achieve. It became clear that neither could meet their long-or short-term goals without the customer. What they were discovering was that in fact they had a lot in common.

Stepping back to consider their individual objectives as well as those of their competitor had unintentionally created a context for pursuing the partnership. They needed the customer and therefore each other.

The lesson I took away from this event was that it is important to look at the bigger picture early on. It is important to have thought through what you most want to achieve both as an organization and then as a result of this endeavor. By being open and candid about these issues, you are making your intentions clear.

13. Planning poorly

Considering all of the partnerships, alliances, and collaborative efforts I have been associated with, I have become more and more convinced that planning makes the difference between success and mediocrity.

Whether you are planning the initial coming together, the overall intent or reason for the effort, the implementation of the work that will occur as a result of the effort, or the process you are using, don't underestimate the need to plan and think through what needs to be done.

In the best of situations you will be planning with your partners. If joint planning is not feasible, then at a minimum involve your partner(s) in getting input as to where you take the effort. A side benefit of doing so is that you will likely engender trust and confidence that you have the best interests of all sides in mind.

The unplanned coming together at best signals to your constituents that you may not know what you are doing or at worst are not to be trusted.

14. Lacking a shared vision

Far too many of these efforts suffer for lack of vision. I don't mean that esoteric, ethereal kind of vision statement that really isn't useful. What I'm talking about here is the value of working together to create a view of what is possible as a result of the effort. Once there is understanding about what you are individually and collectively trying to achieve and what areas of mutual benefit might be possible, you must then be clear and specific about what your overall goal for the collaboration is.

I want to underscore the notion of *shared* vision. This vision or over-arching goal needs to be one that excites the group and is clearly worth pursuing. When players change or when the going gets tough, bring back that vision as a way to reenergize and motivate the group to keep going.

As you work toward articulating the vision, you are in fact creating a sense of community or commonality within the group. As such, your vision becomes the context for moving forward and investing whatever energy is necessary to make it real.

Lastly, make sure that the vision is stated in terms of "what" you will achieve versus "how" you will achieve it. There will be plenty of time to figure out how you will do it. For now, focus specifically on what you most hope to achieve as a result of the collaborative effort.

15. Allowing unhealthy egos to get in the way

During one of my workshops, a student brought up the issue of ego. In a very thoughtful way, she told the class that developing collaborations and partnerships was her primary assignment. This woman had years of practical experience bringing people together over very complex and contentious issues. As she continued to speak, it became clear that she understood this well.

In a tactful way, she proceeded to say that for her it was simple. If you could keep the big egos out of it, collaboration would be easy.

Following a round of knowing chuckles, the group began telling their individual perceptions about the negative impacts they had witnessed in the workplace as a result of out-of-control egos. In particular, we began to examine the role ego might play in collaboration.

Many, including myself, have strong opinions about ego. While I can't prove it, I have always suspected that an unhealthy ego plays a significant role in derailing leaders, stirring up conflict, and engendering difficult working relationships.

For me, unhealthy egos need to be center stage and to control situations, and are characterized by a lack of openness and conciliation and a hesitancy to let go or change a position even when it is for the greater good.

While this book is not about analyzing ego, I can offer this. If you have a role and something to say about who you put in charge of collaborative efforts, watch out who you place in those situations. The very best technical expert may not be the right person for the job.

Look for someone who can display a little humility, see and appreciate the overall situation, and who has a track record of building and sustaining successful relationships over time. I suspect you have never seen those attributes in a position description! Just know that many efforts fall off track or get stalled because of the behaviors of individuals who are unable or unwilling to see things anyway but their own.

When dealing with individuals in the group who are displaying unhealthy ego, look for ways to mitigate the negative impact. One method I have used is to make every attempt to meet the need of the problem individual to the extent possible. That is, if that individual wants to take a lead, I offer the lead to him or her. If such individuals need to have their name on things, I welcome that. What I do not allow, however, is unhealthy disruption of meetings or grandstanding. To control those types of behaviors, use jointly identified ground rules and get agreement that the group is responsible for enforcing the ground rules in real time during meetings. While this works well most of the time, there may be occasion to work directly with individuals privately, or to engage the facilitator to help manage the difficult individual.

Lastly, if any of the unhealthy behavior listed here sounds a little bit like you, Chapter 3 is for you.

16. Clashing culturally

Culture is the attitudes, mind-sets, norms, and beliefs that permeate the operation of the organization. This is the stuff that you don't see in the organization chart or in the policy or procedure books. Culture is how things *really* work within the confines of every organization.

Culture is real. Whether it makes sense or not, whether we agree with it or not, the culture of an organization will impact what happens with any collaborative effort.

To the extent necessary for your particular effort, seek to understand the cultural aspects of the participating organizations. Some of the questions you may need to consider are: How are decisions made? How much autonomy to make commitments do the players at the table really have? What level of involvement does both your and others' leadership need to have? How likely are plans to be blessed versus being rejected? How important is this effort in the overall scheme of things? Who are the formal and informal leaders and how should they factor into the effort? What external organizations or boards might influence their direction and what happens?

By having a sense of this type of information, you will be better able to plan and execute work as you go along. Do not be surprised when issues surface out of what seems like nowhere or unexpected oversight or delay happen. If this occurs, chances are you are dealing with some cultural aspect of either your organization or that of your partner(s).

There was one particular collaborative effort that helped me consider the impact of culture. In this case, after having invested significant effort, resources, and time, I had to learn this lesson the hard way. The situation involved a particular natural resource agency and a set of community business owners and residents. It seems they had been trying for quite some time to open a visitor's center for the many tourists that came through their community via a nearby interstate. Both the community members and the agency representatives were eager to encourage visitors and wanted to facilitate the dissemination of information, maps, and other items of interest about the area.

The collaborative effort came together rather easily since the context of providing visitors information was shared. One community organization offered the perfect location that came with office space, a reading room, restrooms, and great access. They made plans, ordered materials, assigned people, and the center was just about ready. As the opening date approached and during a group meeting, the community leader in charge of solidifying the deal for the space stood up and dropped a bombshell. The only thing that still needed to be done, he said, was to run the decision to turn the space into a visitor's center by the board that controlled the real estate to be used. Up to that point, no one knew there was a board involved.

Sure enough, the newly appointed board chair, hearing of the decision for the first time, readily and heartily refused to allow that space to be used in that way. The deal was off as he had other plans for that space.

The community member had failed to consider the long-standing culture of the board. As it turned out, the board had a long history of giving all decision making authority for real estate use to the board chair. While the board chair did take input from the rest of the board, his new appointment had not included information about this particular activity. He had been caught off guard and didn't appreciate it. Had the community member done his homework, he might have been more sensitive to the change of leadership that was in process for months before the transition actually occurred.

We have all seen the well-crafted efforts of committed groups undermined for no apparent reason. What is generally happening in such a situation is that there is some reason that the culture, leadership, or politics of the organization is unable or unwilling to support the continuance of the effort.

The lessons are obvious. Think hard up front and throughout about whom your stakeholders are, who can help or hurt you, and how you will keep people informed along the way. Lastly, don't underestimate the power of culture.

17. Lack of realistic expectations/milestones

I believe that a discussion of possible pitfalls would be incomplete without some word about implementation. Clearly the start-up, the approach, the vision, and the careful development of relationships are all critical factors to the overall success of your efforts.

The reason we all do this work, however, is to get to results! By the time you have arrived at the place where you begin to work on the implementation, you are proud of the progress, hopefully proud of the trust and relationship that has developed, and maybe even comfortable with your new partners.

The warning here is don't get too comfortable. The implementation requires just as much focused effort, planning, and attention as the beginning. Be prepared, knowing this phase may even require *more* attention.

A fairly common error you will want to avoid is to get to the implementation phase and then fail to get very specific about who will do what, by when, what the deliverables will be, and how you will track and monitor progress and success. When you get to this point, take care to think through what is really achievable and how it will be done.

I know of no better way to implement than to use a disciplined project management approach. It is crucial to specify exactly what the work or project milestones will be, who will be responsible for completing the work, how much resource and time will be required to deliver, and what to do and who to inform when a change occurs.

We will discuss this more fully in Chapter 2.

18. Lack of collaborative expertise/leadership

While we will address the issue of capacity more fully in Chapter 4, it is necessary here to point out how the lack of expertise and leadership tend to impact collaborative efforts.

It becomes more evident as time goes on that the level of skill and expertise required to set up, manage, and maintain collaborative work is significant.

While it would be useful, it is not necessary that those given the responsibility to represent their organizations in this critical work are social scientists, or expert facilitators. It is, however, important that they have a good grasp of group dynamics, communication, listening, and dialogue skills. Basic facilitation skills serve as a useful, practical tool for their use.

Perhaps the single most important attribute of successful collaborators is their ability to lead. Regardless of where they sit in the organizational hierarchy, you should consider: Do they tend to garner followers? Are they respected? Do others seek them out for advice and counsel? Is there a willingness to challenge the status quo and to make things better?

When you have the opportunity to influence the selection of those who will lead your collaborative efforts, take care not to give in to the tendency to only consider content or technical expertise.

Aside from the hard and soft skills it takes, the attitude with which one approaches this work matters. Think carefully about the person you are putting front and center to do this work. What you need to look for are those who have an open, flexible, curious, willing spirit to pursue what they believe in. Think about coupling the technical experts with the more socially adept. Understand that you need a good combination of technical prowess and human interaction skill. The bottom line: take the selection of your collaboration experts seriously.

19. Lack of follow-through

It is a challenge to clearly articulate the fragility of trust and how every action taken between partners or potential partners, particularly early in the relationship, is meaningful.

As you walk that pathway toward building a trusting relationship, do what you say you are going to do, don't make promises you can't keep, and keep track of what is happening. The easiest way to raise doubt about your sincerity or intention is to fail to deliver on your commitments.

My organizational philosophy is to under promise and over deliver. Consider and be explicit about what your philosophy is. Whether you are intentional about it or not, whatever you do will send messages to your partners about your intention and trustworthiness. Steven Covey says that if you want to be trusted, be trustworthy.

Later we will discuss the need to establish systems to monitor progress and ways to stay on top of what's happening.

20. Failure to engage adequate involvement and support of key decision makers

Let's be honest. Unless you work for yourself, you are part of a bigger system. While you may operate rather independently in most things, it is a big mistake to underestimate the need to have sanction for what you are doing. It is likely that you are representing your organization, making commitments for the organization, and being the spokesperson for the positions and thinking of your agency or firm. As such, carefully consider who needs to be and stay informed about the progress you make, who might help the effort by their involvement, who should create a cultural bridge between the parties' organizations, and who will be a good arbiter for conflict as issues arise.

The presence of senior leadership is sometimes useful as a symbol of the level of commitment of your organization, and can serve as the contact for their peers at the other firms. While it isn't necessary for leadership to be present at every meeting, they can be useful at the start and during recognition of major milestones and accomplishments.

3

Mind-set Makes a Difference

As a man thinketh, so is he.

—Proverbs 23:7

This word of wisdom especially applies to collaborative work. I strongly believe that our attitudes, mind-sets, and beliefs fundamentally drive our behavior.

Regardless of how hard we try to mask our true beliefs, it is impossible for our behavior not to be impacted by what we think and believe about people or situations. What is even more interesting is that our behavior drives our results.

What this simple but elegant truth means to collaboration is also rather elegant. Whatever we think about those across the table, whatever beliefs and attitudes we hold, cannot help but spill out in the way that we behave towards them. Is it any wonder then that our behaviors drive our results?

Let's be specific here. If we are trying to get to a place where the exchange of value between people can happen, the attitude and beliefs we carry around with us about individuals, trust, past behaviors of the players, the impossibility of the barriers—whatever it is—will leak out in the way we phrase language, our body posture and gestures, even our handshake.

If there has been a long history of not getting along with those cranky environmentalists or those unreasonable developers, it will show. If you are engaging in collaboration because it is politically correct or mandated, but you've made up your mind about the decision or direction you will go, it will come across. In that case, don't be surprised to find push back, lack of commitment and engagement, and ultimately failure.

It is important here to step back, think, and be honest with ourselves about which beliefs and attitudes we bring to the table. Am I willing to suspend my assumptions in the interest of an effective collaboration? Is it possible to reframe how I think about the other person or the situation? Is it possible that I don't have all the facts and that I might learn something that might alter how I think or what I know? What is my margin of openness to allow the collaboration to influence what happens and where we go?

If the relationship has a negative history or an individual has a reputation for being difficult, can we start over and work from this day forward? Would it be helpful to ask others if we can start anew?

These questions are not easy to answer but are worthy of consideration, particularly if you are mystified about why things aren't moving as they should, you get stuck, or it looks as if you've reached an impasse.

Remember, if you don't like the results, some would say change your behavior. I say, change how you think about the situation—change your attitude and how you think about it.

The model offered below illustrates this concept and may be illuminating as you examine your attitudes, behaviors, and results.

Link between Attitudes and Results

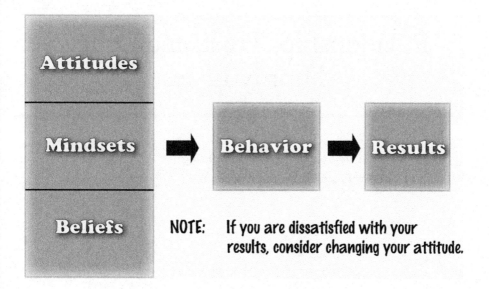

NOTE: If you are dissatisfied with your results, consider changing your attitude.

Lastly, whether we intend it or not, people sense how we feel about them. If you want to change another's attitude about you, change the negative attitude you carry toward them.

4

Relationship, Trust, and Other Thorny Issues

A fool finds no pleasure in understanding
but delights in airing his own opinions.

—*Proverbs 18:2*

For all the angst about trust, it really is about exhibiting integrity, intentionality, and consistency throughout any relationship. While it sounds simple, there is a lot to this task of building trust as a basis for relationships.

Mutual trust is the belief that we can depend on each other to achieve something we both believe in. When we trust, we become vulnerable because we know we can't control the actions of others. As such, let's accept the element of risk that is present and acknowledge that whenever we enter into relationship, we risk being disappointed if things don't work out. We can handle risk better when we know it is there and have weighed the cost and benefit of taking that risk.

As we begin collaborative efforts, perhaps we should mindfully weigh the risk associated with investing in relationships. Perhaps we should clarify in our own minds how willing we are to invest the time and energy required to build relationships. Perhaps we should consider how willing we and our organizations are to be dependable and deliver on our end of any resultant commitments.

Let's think through how we can become intentional about building the bonds of trust and how we should approach the creation of these fragile and enormously useful bonds.

Steven Covey talks about the notion of the emotional bank account. That notion has particular relevance in the collaboration arena. The way Covey describes the emotional bank account is quite simple. He says that whatever the level of deposit of goodwill has been made into the emotional account between individuals minus the withdrawals of poor behavior or other negatives equals the balance of tolerance, forgiveness, and relationship.

When you apply this notion to the collaboration arena, it is easy to see how the coming together of strangers with a common interest starts with a clean slate or zero balance in the account. When viewed this way, it makes perfect sense that the object at the outset is to make substantial deposits of goodwill.

Goodwill is not schmoozing or smiles all around. Rather, goodwill is framing conversation pleasantly, listening with interest and the intent of learning; actively engaging with others to find commonalities; using humor; being aware of and sensitive to cultural preferences and differences; and disclosing that which is useful and relevant about you, the situation, and the organization.

Goodwill is exhibiting propriety in the way we speak, dress, and behave. It is honoring the conventions of the place and people involved. It is slowing down to absorb the nuances of what is being said and withheld. It is respecting the intelligence and perspective of others.

The result of establishing goodwill is rapport. When we have rapport with someone, we sense that our point of view is accepted and that at some level, they understand us. It is as if we have connected mentally and emotionally and are on a similar wavelength with another.

Building and having rapport does not necessarily mean that you are in agreement about anything but rather that you understand where others are coming from.

When we work inside organizational and functional lines, our boundaries and expectations are fairly straightforward. We know who we report to and to whom our loyalty and allegiance belongs.

Collaboration involves a very different kind of engagement. These kinds of relationships are trust based. Without formal organizational lines or rigid hierarchies, goodwill, trust, and rapport provide the basis for partners to respond together to what is before them. Being able to respond to that which is new, different, unexpected, or changing is essential when pursuing creative solutions. In collaboration there is no forcing function other than respect, collegiality, integrity, and commitment to possibility. Because this is so, the establishing of rapport and goodwill is foundational to moving forward. Indeed, whatever creative, sensible solutions result from the interaction are likely to diminish without the immutable bond of trust and relationship.

If the group of participants is not new, and there is a history of relationship among some of the players that may not be conducive to collaboration, be intentional about reframing the relationship. Rather than pretend the history does not exist, it is better to acknowledge where you've been, take ownership for your contribution to the problem, state your intention to work in a more cohesive way, and ask for and work to get commitment from people to join you in creating a new relationship. In doing so you are exhibiting your goodwill and intention to create a different result.

Lastly, on the topic of thorny issues, I offer the following. More than a few times, I have had an earnest student ask me what to do when there are people at the table that are frankly impossible. They are deemed impossible because of the personality, behavior, and/or attitude they bring to the table.

Most interagency collaborative efforts don't have the forcing function or comfort of clear boundaries and authorities to ensure they get done. In fact, what you are primarily trying to do is trying to influence situations without solid sanction or formal authority.

I invite you to consider how influence occurs. There are different types of power that enable one to exert influence. The first is positional authority or the power affiliated with position. This type of power is the type we're most familiar with, and, frankly, if it worked well, it would be the preferred and surely the most direct method.

Any great leader will tell you that positional power only goes so far. Indeed, if abused, positional power engenders what I call malicious compliance. The notion here is, "OK, you're the boss, so I'll do what you want." Not much buy-in or commitment—only compliance. If taken to the extreme, it can become malicious and lead to sabotage.

Another type of power that assists in exerting influence is the power of competence. That is, if people sense that you are competent and know what you are talking about, you are more likely to influence them by what you have to say.

A third kind of power is the power of personality. One is able to exert this influence because of an ability to get along with others and build trust, rapport, and relationship. This type of power influences people because you are pleasant and easy to work with, and they sense you have their interests at heart.

The key here is to understand the limits of positional power and to work to build your ability at applying your personal power. Personal power is a combination of your position, personality, and competence. The experts will tell you that the most effective way to influence people is to develop and use personal power.

When attempting to deal with the impossible individual, consider the following: Have I used personality, competence, and position appropriately? Have I looked for ways to honor and respect their desires and ideas? Has the person been invited to share his perspective or might he feel disrespected? Is the context for the work you are pursuing clear and shared? Are the roles and procedures you are using clear? Have you set up and are you honoring group ground rules and norms? Does the group have a track record of consistently working through conflict as soon as it arises?

If you can answer affirmatively to these questions then consider what, if any, options exist for changing the makeup of the group. The makeup of the group pursuing the collaboration is important. Where possible, work hard to cultivate willing and committed people and remember it is easier to do that sooner rather than later.

The key learning here is this. If you are leading collaborative efforts, you have a lot to do concerning the issues of trust, rapport, relationship, and people. Issues can be thorny and challenging. While those kinds of issues may not be what you bargained or signed up for, they will in the end be either the glue that holds it all together or the vinegar that aggravates or stymies progress.

5

A Proven Approach

○ ○
The wisdom of the prudent is to give thought to their ways.

—Proverbs 14:8

Up to this point, I have talked at length about what collaboration is, what the pitfalls and traps can be, and how important the issue of relationship and trust building are. As I move into the specifics about what works well and what doesn't, what the patterns of progress seem to be when things go well, and about which areas to pay particular attention to, I offer the following insight and advice on the various aspects of the collaborative process.

The Process

It is hard to overestimate the value of having a well-thought-out and well-designed process for your collaborative efforts. The use of facilitation is paramount to ensure that the meetings associated with the effort are based on sound, jointly created meeting outcomes, a time-bound agenda, and a process for raising issues and managing discussions.

The root word of facilitate is the Greek word "facile." The meaning of the word is "to make easy." To that end, the role of a good facilitator is to enable the work of the group to occur in a more cohesive and unobstructed way.

Other benefits of using facilitation are to help identify and remove obstacles to the functioning of the group; to ensure the group dynamics are tended to; and to ensure clarity of where the group has been and is headed.

Another reason for having facilitation, particularly if there is distrust, conflict, or tension in the group, is that all participants should view the facilitator as neutral to the content but committed to the success of the process and all of the individuals involved.

Many organizations are realizing the value of skilled facilitation and have internally trained people who are capable of managing the process. In most cases, internal facilitators are fine, and since they are close to the work, it is often convenient and cost-effective to use them. When using facilitators, make sure that their role is clear to the group in order to minimize the appearance of bias. If you are facilitating, make sure the group clearly understands when you are in the role of facilitation and when you are in the role of participant. It is easy to get those roles confused.

If particularly high tension, conflict, or distrust characterize the situation, it may be necessary to bring in third-party facilitators who the group is more likely to perceive as unbiased and neutral.

If you are selecting facilitators for your collaborative effort, look for one that is knowledgeable about and skilled in managing group dynamics, is able to manage multiple personalities without offending people, and one who can think on her feet, is flexible to the needs of the group, and is willing to challenge the group when necessary.

The Start-up

It's highly likely that you didn't go to school to learn to facilitate the bringing together of people. It is ironic that most professionals spend years learning their area of technical expertise, whether science, engineering, ecosystems, accounting, archeology, or construction, but no one told us we would be responsible for developing rapport, building trust, finding common ground, or building mutually satisfying solutions. In fact, that was likely the last thing on our minds as we entered the workplace.

We know now that those who are able to build and sustain long-term relationships are in high demand. Conversely, we also know that even for the most technically astute, not being adept at these things may prove to be career limiting. How times have changed!

Clearly, the end result depends not only on your ability to bring people together but making sure you bring the right people to the table.

Up-Front Stuff—Before You Begin

I advocate serious consideration be given to the selection and invitation of your partners and/or stakeholders to the table. My bias is that way before you sit down at that first meeting, you spend time thinking through just who should be at the table with you. I advocate including those who think like you and those that don't. Since we tend to get comfortable with those who see our plans and agree with our positions, I believe in intentionally selecting the members of the group in such a way as to ensure a balanced view.

Time is well spent planning and thinking about questions like: Who has expressed interest in this issue? Who might this effort impact? Who is likely to have different ideas about how this goes? Who could be hurt or helped by this action? Who has the power to stop or interfere with this effort? Who has invested significantly in the way it is now? Who knows about the likely future of the issue?

It is hard to overstress the need to err on the side of inclusion, particularly at the beginning. One way to make sure this happens is to create your original list of invitees and then vet it with others who are familiar with the topic or issue. By doing this, not only are you modeling collaboration, but you're also likely to identify gaps in your own initial assessment.

Once you have a good sense of who should be involved, it's useful to conduct a bit of an analysis about the potential participants or stakeholders. A tool I have created for use in this assessment is included in Chapter 9: Tools for Action. The matrix I use is something I call a Stakeholders Analysis. The intent of using the tool is twofold: 1) to arm yourself with relevant information about those coming to the table so that you can design the initial meeting to be most effective and 2) to find out how much information you already know, what your don't know, and what information gaps exist. By identifying what you don't know, you are better able to create a meaningful set of questions from which to start.

The type of information about your potential partners this assessment will reveal are things like: What is most important to each stakeholder around this particular issue? What is the history of any relationship you may have had with them? What is their incentive for working with you? How would you define the current level of trust between you? What special skills or knowledge are they bringing to the table? What strategies could you use to engage with them?

Many of my students and clients have found this up-front assessment to be very useful as a starting point. For example, if you find that you are not aware of what incentive exists for them wanting to work with you then you know that you will need to make space for that topic to be discussed. If you designate the level of trust to be neutral or nonexistent, you will make sure that you plan for adequate time for relationship building at the start. Conversely, if you designate the level of trust to be low, you know that you will need to address the reframing of the relationship.

Planning is paramount to ensuring a good start-up. Another tip for having a fruitful first meeting is to personally contact the players prior to the meeting. By seeking their input to setting meeting objectives and making sure people know why they are being invited and what to expect, you create a sense of comfort and send a message that you are respectful about their time and how you will be using it.

Earlier we talked at length about the need to invest time in relationship building. What is important to think about during the start up phase is that everything you do is either building up or breaking down the relationship. No action at this juncture is neutral. Until you build mutual trust, the group is evaluating and interpreting the cues you send. For example: Are meetings started and ended on time? Is time respected by having a good agenda and sticking to it? Are people listened to or cut off? Are ground rules established and followed? Is rapport being established? Is the meeting climate comfortable and conducive to exploration? Are notes taken and shared following the meetings? Are intentions stated clearly? Do we know where we're headed? Surely, there are many more cues, but the message is this: take care to do what you can to be explicit and intentional about what messages you want to send. Remember, in collaboration there is no forcing function to stay with the program. When people truly engage and stay through thick and thin, it is because they feel committed to something greater than they are. They can't get there until they feel you are someone with whom they want to do business. They can't do business with you until they know who you are and that you will operate with respectfulness and integrity.

The Issue of Time

A common error I have seen way too often is the underestimation of how much time the start-up ought to, and indeed does, take. In the interest of efficiency, it is easy to miscalculate the amount of time needed to seed relationships, discover what each of the players are looking for, how each might benefit, develop a shared business case, and jointly set up group procedures.

In the consulting world, I caution my clients to be willing to go slow to go fast. What that means for collaboration is that you take the necessary amount of up-front time so that you can be efficient later on in the process. Later in this chapter I will discuss my best estimates of how long a good start-up typically takes.

The Four Phases

Below is an illustration of a model that took shape as a result of numerous years' worth of designing and facilitating collaborative efforts. Upon reflection about what was going on when efforts were successful, I came to recognize a relatively predictable set of milestones groups passed on the way to their destination. As I continue to work with groups, it becomes easier to predict the phases or to use the model as a diagnostic tool when efforts stall.

It should be noted that it is not uncommon to get stuck in one phase or another, to skip a phase, or to ignore one of the phases. When this happens, you need to backtrack, refocus, and get back in sync with the appropriate phases before moving on. I offer the model as a construct to help illustrate the predictable phases of collaborative efforts.

The Four Phases of Successful Collaboration

Phase 1: The Exploration
Phase 2: Making It Real
Phase 3: Set Up Systems to Ensure Implementation and Effective
Relationship Management
Phase 4: Monitor Progress and Adjust as Needed

Phase 1: The Exploration

Phase 1 is the start-up and all of the activities associated with beginning a collaborative effort. This is where a self-appointed or designated leader makes the decision to call constituents together. The purpose may be to meet mandated participative requirements to include the public in actions that affect their communities; to seek out opportunities for growth and expansion; to meet the needs of a customer or customer set; or any of hundreds of other reasons.

Whatever the reason, this is the first part of the engagement. The word "exploration" is quite intentional. The assumption that underlies the use of the word is that at this point no one really knows whether the effort is worthwhile, where it will go, or whether there is potential gain for each of the players. Clearly, the person calling the start to the effort has some notion about why he is making the effort, but from a group perspective, nothing has been decided.

I happened upon this word because it seemed to me that when people came together, particularly if they didn't have any basis for trusting one another, they seemed to be protective and hesitant in the initial stages of their conversations. I sensed early on in the process that many unarticulated assumptions were made and were being acted on. What became the norm was guarded conversation, evaluative statements like "I agree" or "I don't agree," or thoughtful silence.

As an experiment, I began to frame this first phase as an *exploration*. The term seemed to free up the thinking and open an avenue for true discovery to occur. It seemed to enable dialogue when the group started from the premise that they were there to explore, to find out whether they had any reason to continue, not to make decisions or agree to anything but to simply consider the parameters of the issue.

It is freeing for participants to be able to abandon that pressure to commit at this early stage. As I continued experimenting with this notion, I also began to see that in the process of joint discovery, ownership for what the effort might become begins to happen. People and ideas are more freely examined; the building on one another's perspectives begins to take place. How freeing for the sponsor not to be solely responsible for pushing only her agenda and ideas!

The exploration phase requires that you allow adequate time for discovery to occur. Discovery involves honest, candid, open probing and disclosing of who you are and who is at the table. What are your individual histories, backgrounds, and interests? What affinities with and hopes for your respective organizations are held? Why are you interested in this coming together? What kinds of similar issues have you had experience with? What is your reaction to the initial issue being presented here?

It may be necessary to make a point here. This exploration or discovery time is not intended to be a free-for-all or a rambling, useless discussion. The purpose is solidly to build a sense of community and to begin the process of trust building and relationship with your potential partners. What I see happening frequently, even when people know and have known each other for long periods of time, is that this kind of probing and resultant dialogue are not typical. It is surprising how often long-term associates learn new information by being willing to slow down, listen, exchange, and explore.

This first phase of building collaborative efforts also involves a lot of tactical but important tasks. The following lists are offered for the purpose of illustrating the types of activities that will need attention as you get started. This list is not exhaustive and for some situations may include more than is necessary. The intent is to emphasize the fact that much thought and attention is needed to launch a successful collaboration.

The initial start of the exploration phase should include completion of the following:

- Identify and vet the potential participant list with others.

- Assess what is known about each potential player (stakeholder analysis).

- Develop a strategy for conducting the start-up meeting.

- Notify the appropriate leadership from each constituency (as necessary).

- Interview/call invited participants to notify them you will invite them and to outline the purpose for the meeting. (This early contact is particularly useful where conflict, tension, distrust, and/or apprehension about the issue or effort are present.)

- Develop an agenda considering inputs received, making sure meeting objectives are clear and specific.

- Engage a facilitator as necessary.

- Set date, time, and location for meeting (if appropriate, a neutral, comfortable, convenient location).

- Invite participants. (A guideline for participants planning for their calendars is a minimum of three weeks prior to the meeting date.)

- Send out the agenda for the meeting.

- Hold initial meeting and make sure there is adequate time to learn something about each player.

- Build in time for examination of the original premise for the meeting. (Often, this becomes the foundation for the shared vision/context that will surface later.)

- Set future meeting dates/times and process for next steps.

- Decide who will handle the meeting notes and who will be responsible for their distribution.

- Consider who else you might need to be involved and/or informed of the groups' efforts.

Once the launch of the meeting has occurred, the groups should next:

- Spend adequate time to discover something about each participant, their organizations, primary objectives, plans, and priorities. Time should be directed at learning what their interest in the issue/s are, what their best hopes and concerns for proceeding might be, etc.

- Identify and acknowledge what common ground might exist.

- Include plenty of dialogue directed at exploring what the overall context or business case for the effort could or might be.

- Make a go/no-go decision about whether the group believes the collaboration is worth pursuing.

- If yes, then firm up the business case.

- Explore what each participant would expect to gain if the business case were realized.

- Share and vet the business case as appropriate.

- Develop ground rules and procedures for how the group will operate, how it will manage conflict, and what the next steps are.

Again, the purpose of providing this level of detail is simply to illustrate the types of activities that need to be pursued and dealt with and to emphasize how much time and attention you will likely need.

Based on my best estimate, I think you should plan for this first phase of exploration to take approximately six to eight months. Clearly, there can be deviation, depending on the size and complexity of the effort. However, this estimate is based on my first-hand experiences with significant collaborative efforts at play.

Lastly, the ultimate product of Phase 1 is a solidifying of the relationships, the building of trust, and the development of a shared context or business case. If these things are indeed accomplished, it should facilitate the forward movement of the effort.

Phase 2: Making It Real

Once the business case is set and accepted and the group has become comfortable with each other, it is time to move on to the next phase. In order to illuminate this phase, I will discuss a specific situation.

I was invited to consult with a group who had already been working together for about a year. The initial conversation with the client revealed that he was the group convener. His reason for bringing a number of federal, state, and local agency officials together was that he had pursued and won a grant involving significant money. This grant allowed him to spend these dollars to pursue completion of community work projects that would benefit their western community, provided the projects were selected and completed using a collaborative approach.

I probed the client for a better understanding of the situation, what had already been done, the tenor of the group, and what he was looking for. He disclosed that they had spent the first year developing relationships and had been quite successful at doing so. When the group was started, many of the players, while living and working in the same community providing similar and in some cases overlapping services, had come together for the first time through this effort.

After meeting regularly for the past year, he was perplexed, because while the relationships were strong, supportive, and thriving, they just were not making appreciable progress.

I began by speaking with each of the participants, and, indeed, they portrayed themselves as a cohesive, supportive group that really enjoyed each other and getting together. Some however were beginning to wonder whether the effort would bear fruit. According to several of the group members, their reason for being together was somewhat clear at the beginning but seemed to be getting vague.

To enable the group to move forward, we focused our effort on defining exactly what they would do next. We began by collectively identifying the criteria they would use to select projects to fund and pursue. Next, we brainstormed potential projects that were likely to meet their stated criteria. Once they applied the criteria against their brainstormed list of potential projects, it became clear which afforded the most leverage and were closest to their criteria.

At this point, they were ready to move on to planning the implementation. Because trust had already been established, the group moved quickly through identifying what they would individually be responsible for and what they needed from each other to meet their deadlines and commitments. The projects they selected would clearly benefit the community, and, as it turned out, the dollars they elected to invest were nearly evenly distributed across the several participating agencies.

As I reflected back on that particular situation, it was obvious that what they had not yet done was to make the collaboration real. What they desperately needed was a way to move into specifics and to get clear about what needed to be done. Until the effort became real and action oriented, they felt they were wasting time. In this case, the goodwill established at the beginning provided the adhesive that kept it together until they were able to focus.

This phase moved quickly because they had already done the work of discovery and exploration and the relationships and trust were sound. The result was a real readiness to put a stake in the ground to move their effort forward.

It was a little surprising how the group was able to coalesce around the real projects in a meeting or two. I would be willing to bet they could not have made the decisions and commitments they made without the all-important foundation that had already been laid.

My client, the group sponsor, was particularly adept at understanding groups, bringing people together, and sensing what was needed next. Once they had selected projects in which to invest the funding, he began asking questions about how they might establish some sort of structure so that the effort would have sustainability and not become personality dependent.

That takes us to the next phase.

Phase 3: Set Up Systems to Ensure Implementation and Effective Relationship Management

One can imagine that at the point the collaborative effort gets specific and real, it would require less effort or get easier. Unfortunately, there are many stories of collaborations that faltered at the implementation stage. This section addresses what needs to be in place to ensure progress, sustainability, and tangible results.

Once the collaboration focuses on results, there are a number of issues that tend to surface. For starters, as commitments to accomplish work are made, the issues of resources, funding, who will commit their time to do the work, etc., move to front and center. Most of the time there is excitement and enthusiasm about the possibilities, but it is not unusual for there to be less thinking and planning for what it will take and who needs to be onboard to make things happen.

Take care to be thorough about the implementation and what you need to ensure success. Another real situation I worked with illuminates what can happen if someone isn't paying attention.

In this situation, the group had invested significant time reversing what had started out to be a contentious relationship. Nearly a year had gone by, and their regular meetings had migrated from difficult and testy to real joint problem solving in the interest of a shared customer. Once they knew what each other's organizations capability was and what they were trying to achieve, they moved rather easily through the second phase of making the effort real.

After much dialogue, debate, and consideration, they decided that it really would make sense to combine one of the functional areas they each staffed separately. The output of this particular function was directed research and the generation of technological solutions for their shared customer. As they looked at it from the customer's point of view, it made no sense to continue separate staffing and what amounted to redundant effort and confusing signals. As they continued to talk openly about possibilities, it became obvious that the customer was shouldering the duplicity, unnecessary cost, and mixed signals. By combining this one function, each could save operational dollars and could streamline the confusion and miscommunication. The benefit could be further expanded by appointing a single project manager for the work who would also be the single point of contact to the customer. Since each had a separate project manager who felt ownership for his contribution, this decision represented a major change and potentially a major benefit for the customer.

As they talked and planned, they went so far as to agree on who the single project manager and contact to the customer would be. They were very proud of what they had done and celebrated over dinner that evening.

Before this particular session ended, one of the group members, sensing that that the group should inform those affected, volunteered to call a meeting back home to let both functional groups know what they had decided to do. As you might imagine, the staff groups did not take the news of this change very well. As the person bearing the news of the change quickly discovered, the individuals from each side had spent years being major competitors. To hear suddenly that their efforts were being combined seemed crazy! Looking back on this situation now, I can see that the staffs were given no context for the decision, and believe me it caused a lot of trouble back home for both sides.

To make a long story short, it took a lot of effort to help the people whose lives would change dramatically both understand and accept what was about to happen. They had to invest much effort and time, and more than once, the members of the collaborative group that had made the decision had to explain, visit with individuals, and backpedal hard to keep things on track. They knew their decision was a good one, but they had made a huge error in judgment and timing.

There is an important message embedded here. Had they made sure to bring the working staff into the effort sooner and made sure that the systems were in place to get and keep everyone affected informed, the outcome would have been less painful and challenging.

I come back to this example over and over and have shared it many times. The learning was costly and yet so valuable: bring in early individuals who are likely to be affected—the earlier the better. In this case, if staffers had been witness to the evolution of thinking from competitors to partners for the best interest of the customer, surely they would have minimized the pushback and confusion. Had the working people, who after all would be the ones to ultimately determine the success of the effort, been engaged early on in deciding what roles they might play and how they could best make this effort work, I suspect the wringing of hands and gnashing of teeth would have been much less.

I also suspect that the ultimate change for the customer could have been made more quickly and could have been more easily implemented had the collaboration team given more thought earlier in their process to the issue of communication with those affected.

Aside from bringing in those likely to be affected earlier, a secondary lesson is this: while it is not necessary to create elaborate systems and complicate things, it is often necessary to think through what kind of support structures make sense and will serve you as you proceed with implementation.

For example, how will you manage the communication within the collaboration group and with those supporting the process as the group pursues work? Should there be a process for regularly updating those who might be impacted? Should there be a well-understood method for bringing up implementation problems that are likely to arise? What about conflicts or snags between individuals? Is there an understanding of how results will be tracked and monitored? How will the group track changes in players, funding, politics, and the myriad of issues that tend to arise?

Now let's turn to other important aspects of Phase 3 and the creation of some level of structure to support managing the relationships and progress that you make. The client mentioned earlier was correct to be concerned about his collaboration effort becoming personality dependent. Most of us know of collaborative efforts gone awry because the leadership changed or because once an individual left there was not enough to hold it together.

Truthfully, in the situation outlined above, my client's personal involvement throughout the entire effort really made a difference. A very charismatic individual, he had a magnetic personality and a strong belief in what the group could achieve together. His personal power really helped the effort along, and for many of the participants, he was the reason they stayed with it. Because the initial relationship building and exploration is so fragile, it is not uncommon for the group to become tightly affiliated with their charismatic leader. There is nothing wrong with this; however, in the interest of ensuring continuity, it is important to make sure there is documentation, on-going support from multiple levels, and the right amount of structure.

To that end, once Phases 1 and 2 are completed, structure the effort well enough so that you all tend to relationships and make sure there is a method for ensuring effective, on-going communication among stake-holders and decision makers. Significant benefit can be gained by giving early consideration to how the relationships will be maintained and nour-ished once the actual work is decided on.

I further advocate that you err on the side of creating the least amount of structure necessary to manage the implementation. The following tem-plate portrays four levels of relationship management and what the role for each level might be. Use it as is, modify it, or use it as a menu to pick and choose from. The key point is to not leave the relationships to chance or to underestimate the broad internal support that is typically required as you move into implementation and the consumption of resources. I might also mention that the earlier in the effort you organize your thoughts around how much relationship management is necessary, the better. That way by the time you are in Phase 3, there is already understanding about who is going to manage and work the relationships.

The Four Levels of Relationship Management

Level 1: Senior-Level Relationship Executive (for each side)

- Establishes the foundation and rationale for the effort

- Makes sure high-level management meets regularly with partners to report progress, identify needs, and provide resources

- Works to build cultural bridge between agencies and people

- Knows the participating agencies or firms well and is willing to meet with them regularly as needed

- Is willing to confront and work through conflict and make adjustments where called on to do so

- Is willing to sanction collaboration upward and to obtain visibility and resources/support as needed

Level 2: Relationship Manager

- Assumes ownership of the collaborative effort

- Has responsibility for developing a clear and compelling business case with the other parties

- Keeps senior executives informed of progress/issues

- Acts as temporary line of communication to the executive if the effort has particular importance or visibility

Level 3: Program Manager/Technology Specialist

- Has overall accountability for the business results obtained via the collaborative effort

- Has overall responsibility for building appropriate team(s) and ensuring smooth operation of the effort

- Is adept at project management, starting up and maintaining productive teams, and working collaboratively

Level 4: Functional Manager

- Has the people and power to execute the project(s)

- Has detailed agreements and performance responsibility to follow-through

Before we move into the final phase of collaborative efforts, let's discuss a few other common issues in implementation.

Changing Players

With today's workplace becoming more dynamic by the day, it is not a good idea to assume support structures will remain solid as the collaboration proceeds. Most of us have seen one management regime or another get replaced overnight. Do not assume that your collaborative efforts are immune to the impact of leadership or other changes in the makeup of the players.

While there is no way to ensure complete safety or immunity from the impact of change, there are a few things you can do to ensure the stability of the efforts. First, if the collaboration is past the exploration phase and has matured to the point of being a real effort, make sure that your management or others who can influence the future of your efforts tangibly support your work. The best way to do this is to bring in new management early and often; document the business case and any agreements made with external parties; work to build bridges between your organizations; and be clear about the value your firm stands to gain as a result of the collaboration.

It is also useful to make sure that as new players or decision makers change or come onboard, they are completely briefed about where you have been, what the context of the collaboration is, how you operate, what their role is, and what you are doing. It is usually best that this updating is done prior to their first meeting and in person.

Managing Conflict

If you almost never find yourself dealing with conflict, then chances are, you're not getting much done. Conflict is inevitable and clearly a part of the collaborative process. You can expect some level of discomfort/distrust, and it is imperative that you recognize the need for skills, tools, and plans to arbitrate the conflict when it happens.

For some reason, many of us avoid conflict and label it as negative. No doubt the effect can be negative, but conflict can be and often is a catalyst for improvement. As you work collaboratively, it is best to assume that you will run into conflict along the way and decide to manage it as it happens.

Managing conflict means anticipating it, addressing it, and working through it as soon as it happens.

Conflict occurs when the expectations of one or more parties are violated. Most of the time what happens is that our expectations haven't been made clear and explicit nor is there a good understanding of the expectations of others. Because this is more the norm than the exception, we have to work hard to slow down and articulate our expectations and ask others to do the same. When expectations are violated and conflict erupts, it is best to quickly open the door for renegotiation and to commit to finding ways to accommodate and adjust as necessary in the best interest of productivity and progress. It is never too soon to open the door to discussion about how the group will address the inevitable conflict.

Since most of us have a preferred style of dealing with conflict, it may behoove us to practice versatility and learn different ways to approach conflict resolution. The Thomas-Kilmann Conflict Mode Instrument is a good tool to use as the group is forming. In this way, there is an open recognition that conflict is inevitable and there are a variety of approaches for resolving issues.

One word of caution offered here. Try to get the group to agree early on that you will work through conflict, missed cues, and violations of expectations before emotions get involved. If you ignore conflict, emotions tend to take over, and then it is much more difficult to deal with. When anger, hostility, and resentment are present the simplicity of renegotiating expectations gets complicated.

The best time to set ground rules around conflict is during the start-up when procedures for the collaboration are being set. It is also a good idea to revisit and solidify your commitment to work through issues as implementation begins.

A few tips for dealing with conflict situations real time are offered. In the beginning, when the group is building relationships, it is common to see a lot of polite behavior. As the group moves into being able to dissect issues of mutual interest, it is highly likely there will be differing points of view. It is at this point that you need set the tone for how disagreement and differing opinions will be handled. If you have done a good job at setting ground rules like no interruptions, being willing to agree to disagree, attacking issues and not people, then bring those ground rules up again. Do not hesitate to specifically bring up prior agreements about what the group will do in the moment when tempers begin to flare.

Project Management

Assuming that you have made decisions within the context of the collaborative effort to achieve some level of work, the issue of how to make sure it gets done looms. If the effort has progressed as planned, getting to the point of being able to develop or achieve something is a landmark achievement. To have gotten this far assumes that there is agreement and a high expectation of payoff for everyone at the table.

Use a disciplined project-management approach because it is the only way I know of that requires the specific, up-front scoping of how much resource, time, and effort will be required to get the work done. By knowing exactly what it will take in resources and time to do the work, who will do what, and what should happen when a change occurs, you have built a sure method for success. By having a project plan, you are also establishing clear accountabilities up-front that you can then share with the collaboration team and those who must support the effort. The project plan will also provide you with a benchmark from which to measure success as the work progresses.

Phase 4: Monitor Progress and Adjust as Needed

In some ways making it to this phase is somewhat like giving birth. To have come together with nothing but potential, created a bond of relationship and trust with others when you don't have to; to have taken the shreds of ideas and possibility and built it into something tangible and then seeing to it that it gets done—these are real accomplishments. So as you reach this phase stop and appreciate your efforts and give yourself (and your team) a pat on the back.

What Phase 4 is about is making sure that you and your partners take credit for what has happened and as necessary have the information you need to make adjustments should they be necessary.

The project plan should serve as your road map for the implementation phase. As you follow that road map, make sure that you intentionally mark off the milestones as they are completed or make changes as the situation or resources change. It is not unusual to forget or neglect to hold those accomplishments up for your support structure to know and to feel good about. This calls for taking the time to go back and inform your internal management, your partners' management, the community, or whoever else has invested in the success of the endeavor. By making sure that others know about progress, you are reaffirming their trust and investment in you, the group, and the effort. It may make it easier for the next group to be able to cite precedent for successful collaborative efforts.

I am a big believer in using tracking systems to make sure you finish what you've planned. A tracking system can be as simple as a spreadsheet that keeps track of which and when tasks are due, current status of work or tasks, and what has been completed. What makes any tracking system useful is sheer diligence and making sure attention is paid to commitments made. Things fall off track and trust erodes when we make commitments and then just assume that "someone" is getting things done or "someone" is paying attention to the details.

Should problems arise due to change or circumstances beyond your control, it is critical that the collaboration team be made aware of what is happening and is ready to make adjustments to the milestones or goals. By knowing the status of what is happening, they can adjust their expectations as well as those of the people who are supporting and trusting them to deliver on their commitments. Any early warning signals you can provide will be appreciated and again strengthen the believability of the partnership.

One of the major reasons that this phase can gets diluted is simply that it is hard to maintain the level of energy and enthusiasm once things are decided. It takes a rare individual who can keep the interest and progress going and be the cheerleader as things get done. Another common issue is the amount of change that occurs during and throughout the process of a long-term collaborative effort. I offer another reminder to make sure that you do not allow your efforts to become personality dependent. Make sure that everything is documented, the necessary structure is in place, relation-ships are managed carefully, and supporters and constituency are informed and onboard at every step of the process.

6

The Relationship Factor

While I have already covered much information on the importance of relationship and trust, I devote this chapter to analyzing the nuances of the role the convener plays in developing, nurturing, and maintaining relationships. Many people I have firsthand experience with have tended to minimize or underestimate how important it is to focus on the role of relationship builder. As illuminated earlier, those taking on the convener role frequently find themselves with enormous responsibility and little formal authority.

To create and foster an environment where people feel comfortable talking about their preferences, knowledge, values, and ideas as well as what they still need to learn is a true challenge, particularly where interests vary and complexity abounds.

We humans naturally tend to assign respect and at times even awe to those who possess what we call charisma. The word "charisma" (from the Greek word *kharisma* or gift), is often used in this form to describe an ability to charm or influence people. It seems to us that for the charismatic, engaging with others comes easy and naturally. I am quite sure that charisma is not a prerequisite for success at collaboration. I know of no specific personality trait or characteristic that by its nature enables ease or comfort with relationships. While I have no scientific data to support it, I suspect that charisma may be overrated. We all know charismatic individuals who at times come across as more engaged and enamored with their own thoughts than with inviting others in. After all, what is required is not simply the ability to charm but more the good sense to listen and assimilate the perspective of others.

When I think about situations where I am comfortable and willing to engage, it is more likely to be with an individual who displays humility and curiosity. Let me be clear. Whether or not you possess the gift of charisma, truly engaging in collaboration calls for more.

When collaboration succeeds, it is largely because the convener is able to take a fresh look at how things get done through people, take reasoned risks, and share responsibility. Perhaps the biggest challenge the convener faces is expanding her mind-set from regulation, position, and enforcement to innovation and open discussion. Remember, mind-set drives behavior. Having an open mind to find out what others think and how they see things will naturally translate to attentive listening and the conveyance of an invitation to participate. Sincerity, passion, and respect for all views emanate from the belief that we are on this journey together and the best resolution needs your contribution every bit as much as mine.

What is also required to flourish then is the initiative to take a proactive stance to invite participation and the patience and fortitude to embark on the rocky journey across the barrier of no trust toward a carefully built set of relationships. It is knowing when and how to build and use your communication, interpersonal, and influence skills to build and strengthen collaborative capability within yourself and others.

For those heroes working tirelessly in the natural resources industry to mitigate endless battles with special interest groups and communities, a key to your success is taking an active role in knowing and building affinities with your communities and making sure your employees do the same. It is learning to share in the creation of options for decision and action where feasible. It's learning to share your role as leader and the flexibility to wear the various "hats," for example, convener, facilitator, or participant, when called for.

Up to this point I have not specifically addressed the notion of cooperation and coordination. Here I speak of not only garnering the cooperation of your partners but also being cooperative. Tangible cooperation is demonstrated by setting and honoring mutual goals and doing what is necessary to comfortably work together to reach those goals. When there is a need for assistance with respective activities, general support, information, and/or endorsement for each other's programs, services, or objectives exists, openly offer assistance. If there is a need to engage in joint planning and to synchronize schedules, activities, goals, objectives, and events, do as much as possible to meet those needs.

When sponsoring or hosting joint activities, model your commitment to the collaboration by intensively engaging in communication and planning so that you make sure there is clear, far-reaching benefit.

A Model for Building and Sustaining Relationships

In the interest of practicality, I offer some information regarding what I would term a logical approach for building relationships. The Wilson Learning Corporation created the material to assist salespeople through the relationship-building process that would lead to sales. In my view, the material has particular relevance to the issue of building and sustaining relationships in the collaborative arena as well.

Wilson teaches the engagement process in a somewhat linear way; however, it does help to wrap a construct around the required steps in building and sustaining long-term relationships. Following is a summary of the steps and what each step entails.

Relate

This first step calls for recognizing when no trust exists and is geared at raising the comfort level of others to interact with you. Relating is establishing credibility, competency, commonality, and trust so that you can get to doing business.

For those working in the collaboration arena, this step is taking the time to establish connectivity mentally and emotionally. Do not underestimate the time required for this step.

Discover

This step involves taking the time to understand the other person's perspective and perceptions. Discovery means taking the time to find out what your potential partners have currently, what they want, and what their notion of "ideal" for your efforts is. The purpose of this step is to help overcome the sense that they don't want or need to be part of the effort. For example, if you are approaching someone to pursue funding for a project, they may not understand the need for funding your project or even that there is a need.

The key to discovery is to understand, from the other person's point of view, *their situation*. To assist you in this phase, Wilson recommends you become adept at different types of questioning and probing techniques. In my view, the open-ended questioning technique is particularly useful because it invites discussion and sharing.

Advocate

In this step, you are finally at the place where you are free to present your recommendations in terms of solution/advantage/benefit versus presenting why you think something is great.

What is pivotal here is to understand that in this model, one must practice enormous restraint. *Do not advocate any portion of a position you might have about the situation or possible movement forward until the group has thoroughly worked through the first two steps.*

Further, once you reach this step, you must demonstrate a real appreciation for how what you are advocating is being received, what reaction you get, and what the others' objections and concerns are.

Support

This step is particularly relevant to sustaining the viability of long-term relationships and highlights the importance of preserving relationships as if your intention is to engender long-term interaction with your partners that is characterized by mutual support and benefit.

Consider every action following the interaction and work to gain the value of long-term relationships. Support the decisions others make, manage the relationship, address and work through dissatisfaction, practice reciprocity, and work to enhance the relationships.

I particularly value this construct because it helps to dissipate the notion that building trust and relationship is random, charisma based, or dependent on the personality of the players at the table. Further, I recommend that you use this model both as a guideline in the beginning to help with the design of the effort and as a tool for redirecting situations when they fall off track.

Some questions to consider in the diagnosis are: Did we take enough time and make enough effort to establish rapport? Have we used a well-thought-out set of questions to help in the discovery phase? Have I made sure to withhold my advocacy until the steps of relating and discovery have occurred? Did I use what I learned during the discovery phase to frame my advocacy? In other words, does the position I am advocating reflect the needs and wants of those at the table to the extent possible?

A discussion on the principles of relating to others and building relationships is offered here as the final bit of advice on this topic. These principles are influenced both by the Wilson Corporation and by my own observation:

Principle 1

Remember that when people first come together, relationship tension is high. As long as that relationship tension is high, it is harder to concentrate on the task at hand.

Should you have a tendency to think of relationship building as an obstruction to getting to the work at hand, remember it as necessary. As soon as relationship tension is diminished, the desire to focus on the task will follow.

Principle 2

To the extent possible, establish and work from a common base of science, technology, customer need, or other information that all parties accept. By incorporating a common base of information, the expertise and knowledge of the players at the table is illuminated and there is more of a chance to find understanding and common ground.

Principle 3

Keep the collaborative effort as close to the work as possible. Doing so will assist in creating context and minimize confusion. Engage around the work both at the table and walking the project/site. It is easier to build relationship when focus on the benefit you expect to gain is visible and real.

Principle 4

Keep the customer and their needs front and center. Invite in the customer as a way of building context and rationale for what you are doing. Position your customer visits as a way to hear firsthand what they are trying to achieve, how they are now accomplishing their goals, and what gaps they are experiencing. Use the information to build context for what your group will be doing.

7

Ambiguity and Conflict in Collaborative Efforts

A gentle answer turns away wrath,
but a harsh word stirs up anger.

—Proverbs 13:3

The ability to deal effectively with ambiguity is to be able to achieve results or make progress in spite of uncertainties. Certainty about the future and the consistency of things is a thing of the past. When you think about it, the only real option we have in this kind of a work environment is to keep one eye on what is going on around us and the other on continually adding value to our organizations. The effect of the choice to withdraw, wait things out, hunker down, or check out is lack of results and frustration.

In collaboration we have to make friends with or at least get comfortable with operating in ambiguous environments. For some, this is an especially tall order and will require the intentional decision to lean into the discomfort of not being able to predict with certainty what will happen next or how certain our desired outcome is.

At the start of collaborative efforts, expect a high level of ambiguity about many things. For example, will the effort prove worthwhile? Will the players be committed? Will there be adequate support to proceed, and will the current operating environment sustain interest and focus? The list goes on. I want to encourage those engaged in collaboration to expect some level of discomfort but also to pay attention to what is going on around you.

Over the years, I have trained myself to become a bit philosophical about ambiguity and change in organizations. I have worked on this because too often I am witness to huge amounts of worry and stress over things that frankly can't be controlled and nearly always turn out to be less dramatic that the worriers are sure they will be. Most of the hand wringing I see is when people use an ambiguous situation as the opportunity to ponder the worst. For some reason, as I work with people across the spectrum from lower-level employees to the most senior management, I see a propensity for individuals in organizations to lean toward a belief that their scenario will surely lead to some doomsday outcome. You can be assured that attitude of doom will restrict creativity and thus progress and the ability move forward.

I think there is a philosophy that provides reasonable help. Most of our organizations are long-standing, well-rooted organizations with a history of producing value in the marketplace. Barring a financial or other disaster of huge proportion, the changes that are occurring are, for the most part, simply aimed at improving efficiencies and minimizing waste. Since that is the case, why not focus on making sure that everything you do demonstrates value? Said another way, why not focus on what you have control over, which is creating synergy and value through partnership? The best insurance you can get to protect your effort and your own safety is to focus on making progress, adding value, and being open to learning from what you do.

With that in mind, I offer specific examples of ambiguous situations you might find yourselves in and a few suggestions for how you might mitigate them. I have also included some questions you may want to ask yourself when faced with inevitable change and ambiguity.

Example 1: What is the likelihood that your efforts will continue to be supported in the face of significant organizational changes and concern about resources and funding?

If you sense that major change is coming and are worried about whether the time commitment or dollars associated with sustaining your efforts might be in jeopardy, here are a couple of things to consider. Take care not to go too far without regular on-going validation that you have support to proceed. Before you make long-term commitments to your partners or agree to do something that will involve the use of dollars, time, or other resources, make sure that you have whatever necessary approval or sanction that you need. Try to get written approvals or document your understanding. Create time in your meetings for all sides to regularly consider their internal and external operating environments and find out what impacts they might have on your effort. Regularly invite in both formal and informal leaders or people who are in the know and willing to share the latest developments in your operating environments. Lastly, be prepared to make adjustments as soon as change happens and remember that even with these safeguards some things are tough to predict or avoid.

Example 2: How stable is the longevity of key decision makers both on your side and with the potential partners?

If you are very uncertain, consider how to keep regular tabs on and anticipate those changes. Should changes in decision makers or key players occur, what is your strategy for making sure the new players continue to support your efforts? What allies should you engage with to ensure there is a smooth transition if and when change occurs?

Example 3: What if key inputs to your decision making or results are not at the table?

In this case, I cannot overstate the importance of making sure you have the inputs you need before anything is finalized. If it means that you have to slow down, it will be worth the aggravation of doing so. To proceed with the knowledge that you don't have all the pieces to the puzzle is irresponsible and can have high consequence.

In summary on the topic of ambiguity, I encourage you to expect and accept that uncertainty is part of the collaboration equation. Consider and be explicit about your assumptions, what is available as resources (or not), and what your criteria for success is. Make space for others to share their assumptions and put their concerns on the table. Understand and account for political, economic, social, and cultural forces/values that will change and evolve. What will undoubtedly be required of you is that you keep your eyes and ears open and work hard not to assume stability of your support, emphasis, operating environment, or players.

A Final Word on Conflict

Throughout this book I have encouraged you to manage conflict early, up-front, and throughout the collaborative process. I also offer the following as it relates to your personal attitude, beliefs, and behavior in conflict situations.

The model depicted below is a tried-and-true method for managing conflict. I like the model because it provides a common language and a way to talk about conflict within your collaboration team. The premise that underpins this model is that when expectations are violated, conflict results. Since our expectations are often implicit versus explicit, violations are natural and some would say inevitable. The message this model illustrates is twofold: 1) that we need to be intentional about clarifying expectations and 2) that we must be willing to acknowledge and take responsibility for our "pinches" or feelings of being violated.

When one considers the demands of coming together, often with different ideas and notions about how things will work, the challenge of making expectations known is not insignificant. Thinking about and making time and space for discussing what your expectations are and understanding what your partners are assuming and expecting from you and from the effort is also fundamentally important. By doing so, we set the conditions for avoiding a good bit of the inevitable conflict or misunderstanding. When conflict does happen and we acknowledge a "pinch," we open the door to engaging in conversation to renegotiate our expectations so that we can return to a productive state.

The model also illustrates that if we ignore our "pinches," we run the risk of allowing emotions to get involved. As illustrated below, once emotions of anger, hostility, and resentment are involved, the "pinch" escalates into a fullblown "crunch," which becomes more complicated to resolve.

The Pinch Model

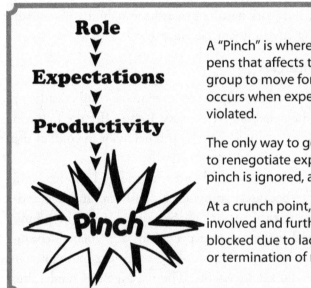

Role

Expectations

Productivity

Pinch

A "Pinch" is where something happens that affects the ability of the group to move forward. It usually occurs when expectations have been violated.

The only way to get back on track is to renegotiate expectations. If the pinch is ignored, a CRUNCH develops.

At a crunch point, emotions become involved and further productivity is blocked due to lack of participation or termination of relationship.

Should emotions get involved, take care not to overreact, particularly at that moment. Get explicit agreement from those involved that they are willing to work through the situation. If emotions are high, call a time out or caucus to let tempers cool down. Offer to bring in third-party mediators if the conflict seems too negative or the consequence of not resolving is high.

Regardless of what is happening around the conflict, always remain calm, respectful, and helpful. State your willingness to work through the issue and take responsibility for your part of the problem.

When there is conflict and the group is floundering, it often helps to bring the group back to the context or rationale for the effort. This reminds participants why they are there and what they are trying to achieve.

While opposition is not pleasant, remember that conflict situations often provide just the right catalyst for improving relationships and situations. If you have set up the expectation that conflict will occur and have defined how conflict will be managed as a part of your group procedures, you will be better able to move through issues swiftly and in a relatively painless way.

Following is a discussion on the principles of managing ambiguity and conflict. Keep these in mind as you work with others to balance making progress with the very real challenges of managing conflict, building relationships, and working in a challenging and dynamic environment.

Principle 1: Expect the unexpected.

Do not get lulled into believing that the scenario you start with is fixed or that what is true for you or your partners today will be so tomorrow.

Principle 2: Listen openly and respectfully to the hard stuff.

Pledge yourself and get your team to commit to early identification and resolution of both real and perceived issues/barriers. Encourage and retain a positive environment, work with skeptics, and frame issues to promote positive dialogue. Insist on civility so that reasonable discourse can occur.

Principle 3: Make up your mind to be an active participant in resolution of issues, take reasoned risks, and share responsibility.

Prepare yourself to lean into the discomfort associated with conflict. Ask and answer—what would it take to resolve this issue? What do I and the success of the overall effort stand to gain if this issue is resolved? What is the cost to me personally, to the collaboration, and to my career of not resolving this issue?

Principle 4: When working through conflict, work hard to stick to the issue at hand, *not* focus on personalities.

Be clear about what you want and ask for what you need. Avoid bantering positions back and forth. Instead, jointly create alternatives or options for mutual benefit. Approach every issue and conversation with an open mind. Know what your hot buttons are and control them! Remember, when you lose your cool, you give away your power. Train yourself to stay calm and remain silent until you can control your tone of voice and your emotions.

Principle 5: When talking through conflict, use "I" statements.

Taking ownership for your own reaction tends to minimize defensiveness and signals that you are taking ownership for your "pinches." Clearly state your intention and desire to resolve the issue. State your *perception* of the conflict and how you *feel* about it. Ask for the other party's perception of the conflict and how *they* feel about it. Try on the other's perspective. Work until you reach what both parties consider an agreement that is wise. Either proceed to resolution immediately or request a meeting in the near future (set a date and time) so that you can discuss and resolve it.

8

"This Is Not the End ..."

"It is not even the beginning of the end. But it is, perhaps, the end of the beginning." These famous words were spoken by Winston Churchill during a speech he gave at the Lord Mayor's luncheon in 1942. These words may accurately reflect where we are today in the world of collaboration. We are not at the beginning. So much work has already been done and continues to be done. There are many, many successes and lessons learned that we can point to. We know many courageous individuals who are out there day after day, year after year, experimenting with collaborations and partnerships and improving and sharing what they know.

We are not at the beginning of the end because there is still so much more to learn and try and do. Perhaps where we are is at the end of the beginning. That is, we are firmly on the road to knowing that there really is no other way to operate successfully in this millennium but to work together. We know that we need each other and that we can't do it all ourselves. We have discovered that staying with complexity and working through the puzzle of ambiguity is richly rewarding. We are individually and collectively gaining a healthy respect for the fragility, utility, and richness that lies within the human experience of doing this work. To relinquish the notion that we have the answers and know best is a major step toward reaching shared vision, the wealth of mutual benefit, and the exchange of value between parties.

So as we come to the end of this book, it is fitting to remind ourselves of why we continue to pursue that illusive magic of coming together to create more than we start with. While I don't play music, I wonder whether we are really jazz musicians disguised. They are the ones who come together with a trust for synchronization. Jazz players bring themselves together and read and watch and listen to one another to find the rhythm of the group. They tap into each other by listening and being fully present in the noise so that they will know exactly which note they can insert at just the right moment to make music and create something not one of them could do alone. They come together not knowing the answer to what the next note will be but rather trusting in themselves and the intentionality of their fellow musicians.

I challenge you to consistently and honestly ask yourself: Am I listening and reading and watching the rhythm of my constituents? Am I pushing myself to be fully present in the noise and looking for opportunities to insert my value to the mix?

On more than one occasion I've been asked: what is the bottom line in making collaboration work? I have considered and continue to think about that question. What I keep coming back to is this: *the bottom line is that whatever the context or purpose of the effort is, whether we engage because we have to or because it just plain makes sense to do so, we are the instruments of our success or failure.* We individually and therefore personally have the power to make or break these efforts to a very large degree. This may be uncomfortable for some, but it's far too easy to exonerate ourselves from that responsibility. I think we are accountable for our results because of the attitude with which we approach our partners, by the respect and integrity we bring to every interaction, and by remaining open to possibility.

The bottom line then is simply to be the best partner we know how to be. We are the best when we are just in our every action, empathetic and compassionate to what is being brought to the table, and when we walk with humility among the issues and the people we are trying to influence.

When I started this journey of writing down the lessons of collaboration I felt driven to provide specific tools, models, practical approaches, and constructs. I trust you will find those, and again I sincerely encourage you to freely use whatever you find here that might be of value to you. Beyond these tools and constructs, however, I hope you trust that you are the real instrument for success. Your attitudes, mind-set, beliefs, and behaviors are the real currency of collaboration.

Should you come across ideas, learning, or lessons not found here or if you want to challenge or encourage what you have found in these pages, I personally welcome open dialogue. We are, after all, at the end of the beginning.

Finally, the last two chapters offer you 1) a set of tools for action and 2) specific case studies to share specific steps and outcomes that occurred with real situations

9

Tools for Action

o o o o o o o o o o o o o o o o o o o o o o o o o o o o o o o o o

I laid a foundation as an expert builder, and someone else is building on it. But each one should be careful how he builds.

—*Corinthians 3:10*

This chapter is a practical tool kit to use as you start-up and manage collaborative efforts. These tools have evolved over time or have been shared with me by various clients too numerous to mention. I would, however, like to acknowledge the fine folks at the United States Department of Agriculture Forest Service, the Bureau of Land Management, and many other organizations whose employees work diligently and tirelessly to make collaboration work. I've had many students willingly share their insight, techniques, successes, and tools. It is because of their generosity and willingness to collaborate with me that many of these tools are presented here.

Some of what you will read about has evolved through collaborative discussions and trial and error. People have successfully used each of these on numerous occasions and in a variety of situations. They have provided and continue to provide specific assistance with the numerous aspects of real collaborations. Following is a list of nine separate tools I have included along with a brief discussion of their intended use.

Tools for Action:

1.	**The Continuum of Collaborative Efforts**
	This tool will help you asses what type of effort you need to pursue before you begin. It is essential to be clear about the goal of the effort in order to plan appropriately. This tool helps you identify the type of collaborative effort needed in order to plan how to move forward.
2.	**The Five Steps for Organizing your Collaborative Effort**
	This is a framework with steps to help plan and organize your effort.
3.	**Stakeholder Analysis Worksheet**
	This is a worksheet for assessing the needs and interests of your stakeholders and/or potential partners before you begin the effort. Use it to determine how much you already know about your potential partners and what you still need to learn. The worksheet helps you determine what kind of information you need to gather up front and therefore where to start.
4.	**The Triad of Collaborative Efforts**
	The Triad model shows the necessary balance between relationship, shared context for the effort, and operating procedures. Use it as a diagnostic tool for current efforts and as a guide to establish appropriate balance for future collaborative efforts. The Triad will help you quickly identify which area may be out of balance in order to focus your time and resources effectively.
5	**Sample Meeting Guide**
	This is a sample agenda for starting up and working through collaborative meetings.
6	**Checklist 1: Reasonableness of Effort**
	Helps you determine if you effort is appropriate and if it has a reasonable chance for success.
7	**Checklist 2: Managing Inclusion and Diversity**
	How well does your effort welcome a variety of opinions and perspectives in your effort? Use this checklist to evaluate your efforts at inclusion or as a diagnostic tool when you experience difficulty.
8	**Checklist 3: A Shorthand Approach to Consent Building**
	Use this tool to clarify your philosophy with your partners and/or for planning the communication model essential to successful collaborative efforts.
9	**Checklist 4: Formula for Success in Collaborative Efforts**
	Use this as a reminder of the basic foundational needs for all collaborations.

Tool 1: The Continuum of Collaborative Efforts

The desired outcome of the relationship dictates the degree of relationship necessary. The degree of relationship required in a large way dictates how much time and effort will be necessary to ensure a successful collaboration. Some issues you will work on require only increased communication with stakeholders. Others demand a much stronger and far-reaching interaction. The continuum is useful in helping you determine how much time and effort you should plan for and what level of relationship you will need to accomplish your intended outcome. The five levels of collaboration are detailed below:

The Continuum of Collaborative Efforts

Level 1: Communication

Level 2: Cooperation

Level 3: Coordination

Level 4: Collaboration

Level 5: Consolidation

Before you begin any collaborative effort, it is important to consider where on the continuum your particular efforts might fit. The type of effort you are intending to achieve will dictate the amount of time and effort you will need to plan for. The higher level up the continuum your effort falls (Level 5 being the highest), the more time and effort you will need to plan for.

Following is a set of characteristics or attributes that define each of the elements along the continuum.

Level 1: Communication

- Individual program or causes totally separate

- Need for exchange of information to maintain meaningful relationships

- Need for clear, consistent, and nonjudgmental discussions

Level 2: Cooperation

- Mutual goals and a need to work comfortably together to reach those goals

- Need for assistance with respective activities, provide general support, information and/or endorsement for each other's programs, services, or objectives

- Policy and customer decisions are typically autonomous

Level 3: Coordination

- Need to engage in joint planning, synchronizing schedules, activities, goals, objectives, and events

- Joint activities and communication are more intensive and far-reaching

- Mutual goals desirable, participants consider each other equals

- Policy and budget decisions still relatively independent

- Program services, advocacy efforts, accountability, and outcomes distinct by agency

Level 4: Collaboration

- Actual changes in agency, group, or individual behavior, operations, policies, budgets, staff, and resources to work together to support the collective goals or pursuits

- Agencies, groups, or individuals willingly relinquish some individuality or autonomy in the interest of mutually beneficial goals or results

Level 5: Consolidation

- Organizational, group, and/or individual behavior, operations, policies, budgets, staff, and power united and "harmonized"

- Individual autonomy or gains are fully relinquished toward adopted common outcomes and identity

---

Key Point: Regardless of the type of effort, the principle of respect, the willingness to seek mutually beneficial solutions and negotiate win-win solutions, and the open sharing of relevant information must be present.

Before you begin any collaborative effort, consider what you are trying to achieve. If, for example, all you need to do is communicate with a certain constituency, you will need to plan for less time and effort than if it were a full-blown collaboration. As you move to the higher levels of the continuum, you will need more time to plan, analyze your stakeholders, and deal with political influences.

Many well-intentioned, potentially high-leverage efforts do not meet their intended result because of failure to recognize, plan for, and address the political factors of each of the parties. When dealing with nonprofit entities, take care to recognize the complexities of boards and the influence they have. When dealing with tribal issues, be aware of the cultural aspects of the interface. When dealing with special interest groups, take care to take the time to fully understand their opinions and what is driving their action.

Lastly, use the continuum to assist you in your initial assessment of what you need to do to start up and sustain the necessary communication and joint problem-solving efforts.

Tool 2: The Five Steps for Organizing Your Collaborative Effort

Step 1: Assess the potential for collaboration.

Step 2: Make sure you have the skill necessary to develop effective collaboration.

Step 3: Design the collaborative process.

Step 4: Implement the effort.

Step 5: Monitor and evaluate progress and make adjustments as
   necessary.

This tool provides a conceptual framework for planning and organizing your collaborative effort. Some find this to be a useful framework for thinking through what kind of up-front work needs to be done and what level of resource may be necessary to proceed.

Step 1: Assess the potential for collaboration.

Step back and carefully consider who the stakeholders in the effort might be. Stakeholders are defined as those who can help, hurt, or potentially stop your effort. It is here that you attempt to clearly define the potential benefit for you and for each of your partners. If you are unable to clearly identify, from *their* perspective, what your partner(s) stand to gain, you may want to contact them one-on-one ahead of time for exploring their interest and willingness to proceed. Another factor to consider at this first step is who the candidate sponsors within your organization might be and to set plans in place for how you will bring people together for the initial and subsequent meetings.

Step 2: Make sure you have the skill necessary to develop effective collaboration.

Think about whether you have the skills and abilities you will need to initiate and sustain the collaborative effort. As a part of Step 2, carefully consider who to select to be the convener or lead for the effort. Make sure the person who will be planning and working the effort is trained in facilitation, group dynamics, and collaboration. If resources are at a premium, you may want to consider sharing the burden of planning and executing the meetings with your partners. Joint ownership of the effort is something you might consider in this step, particularly if your partner has capability and they are willing to share their time and effort.

Step 3: Design the collaborative process.

Craft the initial design for the effort. The results of your initial assessment of your potential partners, the state of the relationship, and what might be needed to build trust and explore the interests and needs of each participant should influence the setting of outcomes for the initial set of exploratory meetings. Take care to intentionally build in enough time to get to know each other, explore possibilities, and discover what you need to know about each other and your respective interests. Lay the foundation of your design carefully and intentionally. At the end of each meeting, do a group assessment of how the meeting went and what you might need to do differently at the next meeting. Be flexible enough to change course as needed and in the best interest of the group.

Step 4: Implement the effort.

This is the critical implementation step. As discussed earlier, this step requires good direction and a good understanding of what is going to be achieved and who will do the work. Do not underestimate the importance of thinking through the implementation steps carefully and thoughtfully. Use project-management planning tools as a way to plan for resource needs and time commitments. By using a disciplined project-management approach, you will increase the probability of success since everything required will be clearly spelled out and well understood by all parties.

Step 5: Monitor and evaluate progress and adjust as necessary.

Track progress, identify implementation problems early, and validate success. This step is important to those who have invested the time and effort to bring the effort to fruition. Make sure that you celebrate each success, thank those who have contributed to the progress being made, and keep your sponsors informed as progress is made.

Tool 3: Stakeholder Analysis

The following worksheet provides a way to conduct an early assessment of your stakeholders. Use this matrix to conduct an honest, unbiased assessment of what you know (and don't know) about your potential partners before you call them together. Where you are unable to answer the questions outlined on the form, highlight these areas as conversation starters and areas to probe during the early discussions.

The first column on the left side of the matrix asks you to identify the specific names of the potential stakeholders. The second column asks you to list the most important issues to that particular person. When filling this column, consider the issue from *their* perspective, not yours. The third column asks you to describe the history of the relationship. Is it nonexistent? Good? Litigious? Trusting? The fourth column asks you to specify what incentive your potential partner may have for working on this effort. Again, consider this question from the perspective of your stakeholder, not your own. The fifth column asks you to designate a High, Medium, or Low as your assessment of the current level of trust between you and that particular stakeholder. Make this assessment so that you can develop start-up strategies that are consistent with the level of trust. For example, if there is a high trust level, you may not need a lengthy time frame for building trust. Conversely, if there is a low level of trust, you may need specific strategies to start over or spend time finding common ground as a basis to build trust. The sixth column from the left asks you to identify what special skills your stakeholder may hold. This assists you in knowing what abilities or skills you may be able to capitalize on as the collaboration continues. The last column on the right provides for your specific identification of what strategies or actions you might need to take to ensure a good start-up and appropriate relationship building.

Lastly, where you are unable to clearly specify information on the worksheet, you should have a good idea of what kinds of information you will need to pursue as you proceed with the start-up. For example, if you do not know what incentive exists for your partner to work with you, it is important to find that out early on. Where there is no incentive, the likelihood that the collaboration will succeed is questionable.

Stakeholder Analysis Worksheet

Stakeholder Names	Most Important Issue(s) to Them	History of Relationship	Incentive for Working Collaboratively	Level of Trust H M L	Special Knowledge and Skills	Strategies

Tool 4: The Triad of Collaborative Efforts

This tool has proven to be very useful in two ways: first, for diagnosing those efforts that might be off track, and secondly to consider what needs to be done to make sure your efforts are designed and set up in a way that ensures a proper balance between the shared vision, the relationship of the parties, and the procedures you plan to use to reach your goals.

The key message imbedded in this model is that in order to ensure success at collaboration, you must strike a good balance of relationship, shared context and operating procedures.

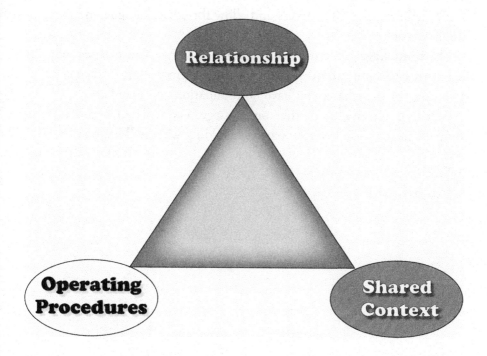

Tool 5: Sample Meeting Guide

Below is a sample of a meeting guide. This sample includes the broad stages of the process, the steps you may want to consider taking during each stage, and a place for you to document any relevant notes for your use as you plan the effort. While this is offered as a guideline, it should illustrate the type of considerations that will be important to build into your meeting plans.

This tool divides the meeting into four stages. These include getting started, clarifying positions, finding alternative solutions, and reaching agreement. It may be useful to think of these four distinct stages as you move through the effort. Remember to allow plenty of time to get started since this is where the seeds of trust are planted.

The second stage, clarifying positions, calls for active listening, remaining open to discovery and understanding, and making sure to summarize agreements and where you are. Typically, this stage requires skilled facilitation to help manage the process and allow for open dialogue and exploration to occur.

The third stage facilitates joint problem solving. You can see why the first steps are so important. If you have done them well, this stage is easier. If you start at this phase, you have no foundation and may falter.

Reaching agreement, or the fourth stage, takes patience and time to complete negotiation between parties regarding what will happen.

Sample Meeting Guide

Stages	Steps	Notes
Getting Started	• Take steps to establish rapport. • Express optimism about outcomes. • Point out agreement/common interests. • Respond to nonverbal language.	
Clarifying Positions	• State the current situation clearly and concisely. • Provide examples or data. • State your goal or desired outcome. • Listen to understand other's goals. • Ask questions to get at needs and interests of each party. • Share "hidden" information about your needs/interests. • Summarize areas of agreement and conflict. • Document areas of agreement and conflict and work through issues.	
Finding Alternative Solutions	• Listen uncritically to encourage open discussion. • Brainstorm possible solutions. • Ask about other's needs/interests. • Ask for alternatives to meet needs. • Suggest alternatives to meet needs.	

Stages	Steps	Notes
Reaching Agreement	• Make reasonable (not one-sided) proposals. • Combine and build on alternatives. • Look for solutions that meet multiple needs. • Identify gaps between needs and solutions. • Suggest alternatives to close gaps. • Summarize and document agreement to ensure understanding. • Keep negotiating if there are concerns. • Clarify next steps before the meeting ends.	

Tools 6–9
Checklist 1: Reasonableness of Effort

The following checklist helps to determine whether your effort is appropriate and has a reasonable chance at success. Answer yes or no for each question to help you determine whether your situation warrants the time, energy, and resources necessary to build a collaborative effort. In my view, you should answer yes to all questions before proceeding. If you answer no to any of these questions, be prepared to overcome any obstacles identified.

- Will the partnership project solve or have significant impact on a real problem?

- Are the goals in the interest of all parties and within the mandate of your organization?

- Are cooperation and collaboration necessary to the project?

- Do the prospective partners *all have* a real reason to participate in the partnership?

- Have you identified all groups needed for the project to succeed?

- NOTE: If a partnership is called for, where does it fall on the Continuum of Collaborative Efforts? What kind of partnership is needed?

Checklist 2: Managing Inclusion and Diversity

Use the following checklist when considering how well you are managing the issue of involvement and inclusion of a variety of opinions and perspectives into your effort, to assess your own efforts at inclusion, or as a diagnostic tool when you are experiencing difficulty.

- Am I seeking to include parties of both interest and place to ensure equity and balanced perspective? _____

- Am I involving people around mutual interests? _____

- Have I established common ground on problems where there is a mix of issues? _____

- Have I accepted and respected the diverse values, interests, and knowledge of all participants? _____

- Am I focusing adequate attention on keeping parties informed on a regular basis? _____

- Have I established our purpose up front then worked at staying focused? _____

- Am I doing what I can to stay focused on interests not positions? _____

- Am I sharing the driver's seat with the other parties? _____

- Have I adapted to new roles as necessary to build psychological commitment? _____

- Am I viewing the process as one of continuous learning? _____

- Am I learning the language, relevant expertise, and experiences of all partners? _____

- Have I fully assessed and worked to build our community capacity, assets, skills, expertise, and leadership? _____

- Am I building on existing networks? _____

Checklist 3: A Shorthand Approach to Consent Building

My clients and friends at the Department of Energy shared this shorthand approach to consent building with me. As I understand it, this was adapted from The Institute for Participatory Management and Planning out of Monterey, California. You may find, as others have, that this is a very useful tool for clarifying your philosophy with your partners. I also believe that this can be an extremely useful framework for planning the communications that are so essential to collaborative efforts. The short-hand approach is as follows:

Whatever you say ...

Whatever you do ...

Whatever you write ...

Make sure that all potentially affected interests will understand these four things:

1. There is a serious problem or opportunity—one that just has to be addressed.

2. *You are the right entity* to be addressing this problem. In fact, it would be *irresponsible* given your mission *not* to address the problem.

3. The way you are approaching the problem—the way you are going about it—is *reasonable, sensible, and responsible.*

4. *You do listen, you do hear, you do care.* If you are proposing something that's going to hurt them, it's *not* because you don't care.

Checklist 4: Formula for Success in Collaborative Efforts

This checklist serves as a set of reminders about what it takes to realize a successful collaborative effort. Use this checklist as a quick reminder of the foundational needs of every collaborative effort and to assess what gaps may be present in your effort.

_____ Have I begun working with the people who will ultimately have to do the work of the effort, and am I bringing them in early?

_____ Have I sold the rationale and benefits of the effort to those who are likely to be affected/impacted by this effort?

_____ Have I sold the benefits to the appropriate levels of management and decision makers?

_____ Have I made sure that high-level management meets regularly with our partners to report progress, identify needs, and provide resources as necessary?

_____ Am I clear about what motivates the other parties? Do I understand the impact of this effort on their business? Do I understand their vision, and do we have a shared vision for this effort?

_____ Am I appropriately managing the interpersonal by making sure someone is responsible for working the communication aspect of this effort?

_____ Am I expecting and dealing with any discomfort/distrust and using an arbitrator of conflict as necessary?

_____ Have I done what is necessary to ensure focus, and have I reworked or adjusted the focus as necessary?

10

Case Studies and Application of Lessons Learned

This chapter provides actual case studies and situations that have taken place. The names of the organizations and players have been changed to protect the identity of those involved. These particular cases were selected because they illustrate many of the principles presented in this book.

The facts of each case are outlined along with the progression of work that was done to help move the situation forward. Where there were particular insights or lessons learned, they are highlighted for your consideration. Following each case, there is a set of tips and lessons taken from the experience. You are encouraged to consider what you might have done in the same situation and are also encouraged to share your insights!

Case 1: Home on the Range—The Facts

Out West there are many ranching families that have worked and farmed the land for literally hundreds of years. Drought conditions over the past decade have stressed many acres of federal land. The disagreement among the ranchers, environmentalists, and the Ranchers' Coalition with the federal agency over the ranchers' right to graze cattle on the land is a long-standing one. As drought conditions have worsened, the battle has escalated into all-out war. The ranchers are convinced that the feds are trying to put them out of business and ruin their livelihood. The feds claim that running cattle on the federal land is contributing to overgrazing and is putting the long-term viability of the landscape at risk. The courts are involved. Litigation and deadlock is rampant. Can they work it out to the satisfaction of both sides, or will the court battles continue?

Progression of Work

It was readily apparent that the long history of mistrust and ill will needed to move beyond the courts and back into the hands of those concerned with preserving both the landscape and the livelihood of the ranchers.

A young biologist went to work for a federal agency, and soon after joining the agency, she learned about the contention surrounding the issue of grazing allotments for the ranchers. Her own management had briefed her about the situation and indicated they would like her to become active in the situation as an agency representative. Since the biologist knew that she had the legal authority to approve grazing permits for the ranchers, she knew the ranching community would be eager to know who she was and where she stood. Her management asked her to work carefully and to the extent possible to try to mitigate the troubling trend of using the court system to resolve the issues. The management at the agency was hopeful that she would become adept at working with the ranching community in a collaborative way to benefit the agency and the ranchers, and to ease the political pressure the Congressional delegation in the region was placing on the agency.

The biologist planned an initial meeting to begin the discussion of the issues. Present at the meeting were the biologist, representatives of the Ranchers' Coalition, several ranchers, and a group of environmentalists who were concerned with the effects of overgrazing on certain species. The biologist in this situation had the role of convener and was not only new to the agency but new to the region as well.

The initial meeting was set up as an exploration. Prior to the meeting, the biologist conferred with several of the technical specialists in her office. The purpose for the initial legwork was to make sure she did not intentionally exclude anyone who might have expressed an interest in the future of grazing rights. Because the biologist called a meeting with her internal group first, she was able to create a relatively robust list of concerned community members and stakeholders.

The first meeting was carefully planned, and the biologist was prepared to play the dual role of specialist and facilitator of the process. The group came together and scheduled the initial meeting for a two-hour time frame. The stated objective of the meeting was to come together to explore the current grazing situation and to jointly consider whether this group thought there was potential for working together to determine the grazing plan for the next three years.

As expected, the ranchers came to the meeting angry and upset and clearly worried that their grazing rights would be further diminished. The representative from the Ranchers' Coalition indicated that it was unthinkable that this agency was working so hard to put the ranchers out of business. The environmentalist indicated that many of the cows were "killing critters" and they should be stopped. Within the first few minutes, it seemed as if the meeting had careened out of control. Emotions were high, and accusations were flying.

To the credit of the biologist, she remained calm, polite, respectful, and noncommittal. She made it a point to hear everyone's concern and then calmly stated that she was new to the area and wanted to fully understand the issues. Her calm demeanor and failure to respond to the accusations and outbursts was just the right behavior for that situation. Following introductions, she took control of the meeting and indicated that they were not there to resolve issues but rather to find out who the concerned parties were and what benefit they might each gain if they decided they wanted to work together on the grazing issue. She clarified her intention of not putting anyone out of business. She went on to say that she herself was from a ranching family and had spent many years on the rodeo circuit during her youth. By disclosing this particular information about herself, she immediately found common ground with her adversaries. One of the ranchers began to question her about the type of ranching her family was involved in, and they discovered they had mutual acquaintances in another state.

By the end of the first two hours, all they had achieved was that the participants knew something about each other, and they decided that it was probably worthwhile to meet again to consider what they could do to keep the ranching families viable and avoid overgrazing to the point of damage to the area.

The first several meetings were difficult but fruitful. After much exploration and discovery, the group decided that indeed finding a mutually satisfying solution to their dilemma was worth pursuing.

A date was set for the group to pile into pickup trucks and drive the acreage together. In this way, they could view the grazing patterns and see for themselves the effect the grazing had on the landscape. Because they undertook the effort to walk the ground together, it became obvious that where overgrazing had occurred, there was little benefit to the cattle and therefore in the best interest of both sides to avoid overgrazing. Once the land is depleted, there is not much hope of grass growth for future years. As such, to overgraze did not benefit either the ranchers or the agency.

Armed with this firsthand shared knowledge, the group was able to identify alternative grazing sites for alternate years. In this way, the cattle could graze for one season in one lot and then move to a second lot while the first lot repaired itself.

A mutually beneficial solution had been found. As the group walked the property and discussed different aspects of their positions, it became clear that they had much in common. Neither party was interested in stalling the issuance of permits because of court proceedings. It made no sense to anyone to deplete or destroy the land. When the cattle were well managed, thinning was achieved for the agency and therefore saved labor costs. In the interest of preventing overgrazing, they would work together to change the grazing patterns and move cattle.

The ranchers learned that indeed the agency was not trying to diminish their livelihood but rather was very willing to issue grazing permits as long as they could protect the land. Those concerned with the issue had successfully challenged their long-held mental models and had been successful at finding a mutually satisfying solution.

Insight/Lessons Learned

What could have resulted in costly and endless court battles, they had instead mitigated through the careful building of common ground and mutually satisfying solution building.

The personality and open attitude of the biologist played a significant role in the success of this effort. The role of the convener is a critical role. In this situation, the biologist intentionally provided facilitation of the dialogue and the process and did not overplay the fact that she had the right to deny grazing rights. Instead, she carefully worked toward a situation where the group could mutually discover that it was not in anyone's best interest to overgraze. While she could have been much more forceful at the outset, instead she conveyed that she didn't know the area well and wanted to make sure she had a thorough understanding of the various aspects of the situation. This display of humility was useful since it opened the door for mutual learning and gave the ranchers the opportunity to demonstrate their deep knowledge of the landscape to her.

Another significant part of this success was when they took the journey together to go see firsthand what the effects of the grazing actually were. By doing this, the situation became real and obvious to everyone. Had they tried to resolve the issue sitting across the table, they would have missed out on a significant and shared-context-setting opportunity.

Tips

Consistent with the principles presented throughout the book, this case offers many helpful hints about what went well. Following are some of the tips I recommend you consider using when there is controversy or a history of difficult relationship with your partners:

1. Plan for time during the first meeting to get to know each other. This step is more than making introductions. Develop a set of questions for each participant to answer. These questions might be something about their background, history, interest in the problem, etc. Do not move too fast to solutions but rather set the stage for mutual exploration.

2. Make the discovery phase as real as possible. If you are trying to solve a problem, get close to the problem. In this case, working together to go see the situation made it real for everyone.

3. Exercise restraint by avoiding making commitments or suggestions too early. In this case, the convener made sure to downplay her authority and instead positioned herself as one who was seeking to learn.

4. Find common ground. By self-disclosing her background, the convener made it easy to connect at the human level. By offering her background in ranching, she immediately connected with the ranchers at a meaningful level.

5. Control your hot buttons. In this case, the convener could have easily and understandably responded very defensively at accusations that surfaced at the first meeting. Instead, she let the ranchers and the environmentalist "vent" their emotions. Rather than try to stop them, defend the agencies' actions, or redirect their thoughts, she remained silent and listened to what they had to say.

Finally, this actual situation evolved over the course of about two years. There were many interactions and meetings. The group in this case started out slowly and gradually moved to deciding a) whether their time was worth the potential payoff, and b) what, if any options might exist to meet their mutual needs. The key lesson in this situation is to take your time, share your intentions, and be flexible and open to the needs of the group.

Case 2: Working with Competitors—The Facts

Firm A, a small, high-tech, five-year-old company, has made significant investments in research and development and as a result, is poised for success. They are ready to go to market except for a specific technology that they need to embed into their product. The cost to develop that particular technology is prohibitive. Firm B, another small company in the area, has already invested in, prototyped, and manufactured what Firm A needs. Firm B is a closely held technology firm that has been in business for eight years. They are known to be independent and successful. They have never met anyone from Firm A nor do they have any history of working with others. Can a partnership work here?

Progression of Work

The initial contact with Firm B had to be made carefully. The marketing director in Firm A had done a fair amount of research about Firm B and had studied information available about their principles, history, and sales materials. Once the information was gathered and synthesized, the marketing director and the senior scientist from Firm A contacted the senior scientist from Firm B to explore whether they might meet to discuss a potential business opportunity.

The intention for the first meeting was to present a win-win business case and to find out whether Firm B might be interested in pursuing a second meeting with their respective management and a potential alliance.

During the first few meetings, both organizations signed nondisclosure agreements, shared their respective strategic and operational goals, and then began to talk about what they might each gain from an alliance. As they talked, it became clear that a business partnership had potential to be quite lucrative for both firms.

The parties took their time up front to introduce the principals of their respective firms to each other, toured their respective work areas, explored potential barriers that could occur, planned out how issues would be mitigated, and set expectations of each should they decide to proceed. As time went on, the conversations increased in their candor and openness and included the setting of go/no-go minimum sales goals for the first and second year.

It was important to both organizations that they be clear about how their respective intellectual capital and rights to the product would be protected; who would be the main contact with the customer and with each other; what role each would play in the delivery of the product; and how either party could back out of the deal without penalty if they chose to do so. At this juncture, the talks were still tentative and in the discovery mode.

On several occasions the group reminded each other that there had not been commitments made and that any agreement would be subject to legal scrutiny.

The relationship aspect of this alliance developed slowly over time. Significant amounts of time and multiple meetings were required to get to know the parties from both sides. They brought in the technical experts who would be primarily responsible for ensuring the quality and quantity of the products early and often and engaged those closest to the work in determining the details for proceeding.

Because of the patience and willingness to take the necessary time to work out the details, this alliance went on to be quite successful for both parties. As a result of this effort, they significantly increased sales for both organizations and cemented a long-term business relationship.

Insight/Lessons Learned

There were more than a few difficult conversations and the building of trust took more time than they planned for. Initially the marketing director from Firm A played the role of liaison and integrator between organizations. His ability to work well with people was a definite asset. The partnering of the senior scientist and the marketing director with a business background provided the benefit of a strong technical and business capability.

A key lesson in this case is to work through the details even if you are still speculating. It is tempting to get hung up on the attractiveness of the technology or to focus on potential sales. In this case, taking the time to work through the potential barriers and then creating options for dealing with different scenarios proved to be beneficial. This work was useful on two fronts. First, it allowed both parties to thoroughly think through what might happen, and, secondarily, the time spent in these discussions had the effect of building a trusting relationship. During the many conversations and hours spent, the players got to know each other and discovered that they had much in common. Their business approach was quite similar, and their founders were similar in personality and in their cautious view of the opportunity. Had they not invested the time to work through their concerns, they might not have been ready to move once they finalized the deal.

Tips

Both of these organizations were technology focused and relatively young on the organizational-maturity scale.

Since there was no knowledge of each other at the outset, trust building and taking the time to get to know the players and their concerns was enormously important. Some of the key tips that contributed to the success of this effort include:

1. Including a marketing and/or business expert in hammering out the details of possible partnerships paid large dividends. It is more likely that the business minds will encourage you to work through the details, and potential pitfalls and risk. Some technical experts get enamored with the technology and don't necessarily think to focus on these kinds of issues. In this case, the business person insisted that both parties sign nondisclosures up-front and that they develop contingency plans for the possibility that issues would arise.

2. When approaching another firm for the first time, make sure you do your homework first. The initial research and being very prepared for the first meeting was important. The initial approach included a well-thought-out presentation that offered a potential win-win case for both parties. Having this initially set the stage for the very professional interactions that followed.

3. In this situation, the personality of the marketing director proved to be very useful. This individual had the personal power and competence to engender trust and confidence in his ability early on. There were many times when the persuasive, open, and helpful attitude helped ease the relationship tension in the beginning and then facilitated movement as they hammered out the details.

4. Notice that several times during the interactions, both parties reminded each other that they had not yet made commitments. It was important in this scenario that the parties were free to explore without committing too soon. Openly stating that there had been no commit-

ments made was helpful and freeing to those in discussion. Taking the necessary time to ensure both parties are comfortable and confident before committing paid off for the partners.

Lastly, this situation could have gone either way. Taking the time to do a complete discovery, build knowledge about each other's organization, and focus on the potential benefit paid off. This situation took place over an eight-month period. For some, that time frame could have been prohibitive. In the end, the time spent understanding all aspects of the situation proved to be very beneficial. As the deal proceeded, indeed they ran into difficulty. Because they had already discussed what they would do to mitigate that situation, they were able to put mitigation efforts in place and move on.

Another key lesson here is that it is dangerous to move forward too quickly or without thoroughly thinking through what could happen and what you will do should something go wrong. If you don't have enough time to be thoughtful about the situation, you may want to reconsider whether you should proceed.

Case 3: Sampson and Goliath—The Facts

A large, growing city in the South is required to subcontract with small business. The city awards a huge construction contract to a very large, well-known construction firm. A condition of the contract is that they portion part of the award to small business. As the contract performance begins, the large and small firm come together to forge their alliance. A lot is riding on their mutual success. They barely know each other, yet they are expected to perform seamlessly. How should this partnership work? Why should the small business trust the conglomerate? How can the large firm trust that the small company will perform? Meanwhile, millions are riding on the success of this alliance. The city expects this to work and seamlessly. What happens?

Progression of Work

The consultant was contacted and asked to design and facilitate a launch session for the start-up of the collaboration between the city and both contractors. The stated purpose of the meeting was to get to know each other, make sure there was a good understanding of the contract terms, and to uncover any issues or concerns either party might have as performance of the contract began.

In preparation for the meeting, the consultant contacted representatives of all parties to find out what specific questions or concerns they were bringing to the meeting and what would be the best use of the time they would have together.

Once those interviews were completed, it was clear that the prime or large company had many concerns about the ability of the small contractor to deliver. Since their reputation was on the line, they wanted to be assured that the small contractor would perform. From the perspective of the small contractor, they needed assurance that the city knew what their capabilities were and that the prime would be good to work with. Based on the data gathered prior to the meeting, the consultant designed in plenty of time for each of the players to discuss who they were and what they needed from each other.

The session began with polite introductions. Following introductions, the consultant asked the participants to state their best hope for the contract performance and their biggest concerns or fears. It was at this juncture that both the prime and the subcontractor shared their concerns. From this point, the discussions because more open and deeper. With continued prodding, the consultant was able to get the group to talk about the costs to their reputation and financial position if they were unable to perform. At one point, small groups went to work to get more specific about the details of what they needed to know about each other, the city, and the next steps. Over the course of two days, they outlined very specifically what they needed from each other to succeed.

As the discussions continued, it became clear that their respective corporate systems for payment processing and for reporting progress were not compatible. What they predicted was very late payments to the small contractor and a less than adequate audit trail for the prime. There were many tense moments and discussion about alternative plans for proceeding. About half way through the meeting, it seemed as if the city might have selected the wrong suppliers for the job! Tempers flared and there were admonitions about how they should have known about the system incompatibilities prior to the contract award.

Finally, the prime contractor, recognizing the potential loss of revenue if this did not work, offered to call in their financial specialists to help define a solution. Once this demonstration of the willingness to engage in joint problem solving occurred, the group was able to engage in creating options for what they might do to work through the issues.

Based on their joint problem-solving approach, they were able to work through the issues and in fact do a remarkably good job for the city.

Insight/Lessons Learned

I have often reflected on this partnership. As I think about what should have happened, clearly the specific details about how the contractors would operate together after award of the contract should not have been a surprise. In the best situation, the city would have worked to ensure that the finalists for the award had the opportunity to explore their compatibilities and potential issues prior to the award.

Given that the process of splitting contract awards between large and small contractors was relatively new at the time, it was understandable that there would be issues with implementation. Upon further reflection, this was a very important collaborative effort. It was fortunate that the city had the foresight to bring the groups together before they started the work.

A key insight with this situation is that it is important to create the forum for authentic communication and the sharing of concerns to happen. At the end of the session, the client shared with the consultant that the consulting skills and third-party aspect of the consulting intervention was critical in helping the group get to the level of conversation they were able to get to. The key here is that when strangers come together, there is a tendency to be polite and to avoid discussion of uncomfortable issues even though they might be pressing. Until this group was able to reduce the relationship tension, they could not get to the task of working through their concerns. They needed to spend much time on finding out who the players were, where they were coming from, and what they needed from each other.

The second insight is that it is necessary to stay with the discomfort associated with the issues raised. Since the customer was present, initially, both of the contractors were hesitant to reveal their concerns to the city representatives. Their fear was that the city might view their issues as a serious barrier to contract performance. In this case, it was important to have a third-party present to facilitate the discussions, ask the difficult questions, and to help create a safe environment for the parties to work out their potential problems.

The third insight with this case is that for this collaboration to work, they needed the relationship, a well-articulated, shared vision for the work, and clear procedures for how things would work (see The Triad of Collaborative Efforts, Chapter 9). In this instance, they had the context (the contract) but very little relationship and virtually no procedures for how things would work. In order for them to proceed and be successful in the collaborative effort, it was necessary to be intentional about building the relationship and the procedures to ensure a successful balance.

Tips

Clearly there was much at stake for the city as well as both contractors. The idea of creating the forum for the "contract launch" was an afterthought and had not been part of the initial plan. The decision by one of the city planners to get the group together rather than just assume that everything would work as planned was wise and key to the overall success of this project. As such, the tips for working situations when virtual strangers are expected to perform work seamlessly are many and include:

1. Do not underestimate the need for relationship building among parties. Once again, it is critical to intentionally create forums and opportunities for people to get to know each other and how each party views the situation at hand. In this case, the direct question about what their

best hopes and fears were coming into the work was important to get on the table.

2. Because there was no relationship and trust at the outset, it was useful to have a third-party design to facilitate the interaction. It is likely that there would have been even more hesitation to disclose their concerns and fears to a city representative or directly to their new partners. Both parties perceived the third party, not affiliated with either side, as neutral and committed to the success of all parties.

3. Once again it becomes obvious that groups must take the necessary time to flesh out their expectations. When the city contacted the consultant, they indicated that a one-half day session would be adequate to the launch the effort. Based on the initial interviews and predicting the need to spend time, the consultant convinced the client to allocate two full days for this meeting and to plan for a follow-up meeting. Reflecting on what actually took place, it was absolutely necessary to have enough time for the respective parties to process what they were hearing and to think through their needs. Having an evening to sleep on what was occurring proved to be quite useful.

4. A key consideration for this effort was having the group realize that they were indeed embarking on a significant, long-term endeavor and therefore needed to meet regularly. At the end of this first session, the group identified regular check-in dates and times and identified who specifically would be in charge of working the liaison between the contractors and the city. The tip here is to ensure clarity about how regular communication will occur. A second tip is to remember that a little structure goes a long way toward managing relationships. By setting up procedures for their work and their next steps, they were putting a structure in place for early identification of issues and a way to track and monitor their success.

Finally, this collaboration resulted in a satisfying and successful contract for the city. While the initial meetings were difficult, they were also fruitful for everyone. The importance of carefully building the necessary framework for working relationships cannot be overstated. Expect a little discomfort, and do not be afraid to ask the questions you know everyone is wondering about.

978-0-595-44719-0
0-595-44719-8

CPSIA information can be obtained
at www.ICGtesting.com
Printed in the USA
FSOW03n1647080617
35031FS